Center and Margin in the Hebrew Bible

Biblical Hermeneutics Rediscovered

The Series as the name suggests will focus on Biblical Hermeneutics, i.e., literary works concerned with methods of interpreting the Old and New Testaments of Bible via different stream of topics like Literature & Poetry, Indigenous Philosophizing, Ethical response towards Ecology, Health & Healing, Science & Technology, Feminist Theology, Sociological approach towards Human Rights, Law & Politics, Arts, History of Ideas, Ancient Civilizations, Cultural Contiguity, Religious Cosmologies & Mysticism, Appraisal of various Theologians, World Peace & Harmony, Global Capitalism, Network Marketing, Cybertheology, Population & Demographics, Epigraphic Studies, Contextualized Education, and many others. We welcome a Mss. on any topic/s mentioned, whether they are original works, scholarly monographs, collections of conference papers, revised dissertations, or translations of historical documents. Through the Series we, the Publishers, are striving to put forward published works that may help Institutions, Academic Bodies, Researchers, Scholars and the World at large in furthering their respective knowledge and understanding on the concerned subject. We welcome your comments on our efforts and further suggestions on how we can enshrine new ray of analysing & explaining the written Texts through our upcoming books.

Biblical Hermeneutics Rediscovered - 24

Center and Margin in the Hebrew Bible

A Subaltern Reading

Shiju Mathew

CWI

Christian World Imprints

First Published in 2019 by

Christian World Imprints
Christian Publishing & Books from India
C-3, Shop No. 14, Ground Floor
Wazirpur Industrial Area, **Delhi-110052**
cwidelhi2017@gmail.com
www.ChristianWorldImprints.com
Phone: +91 11 41526079

ISBN: 978-93-5148-396-0

Printed in India.

Dedicated

to my mother Kunjumol Mathew
who is resting in the Lord.
She instilled in me the godly values

Contents

Foreword

The Revd. Dr Shiju Mathew is an established scholar and theological educator in the field of the Old Testament. As a researcher, teacher and pastor he has been contributing substantially in the field of biblical hermeneutics. Recently, his doctoral dissertation was published and the same was received by the scholarly community with enthusiasm and openness. Now he has prepared a book entitled *Center and Margin in the Hebrew Bible: A Subaltern Reading*. This book is divided into six chapters dealing with the issues of kingship, power, otherness and gender. In our context, these are some of the burning issues which can define and redefine the question of identity of the people of God.

The strength of this book is, according to my opinion, a macro sociological and subalternal analysis which could propose a new arena of Socio-cultural world of the Hebrew Bible. The texts generally present characterization of subaltern communities by depicting the characters within the framework of subalternity. It is significant to note the unique feature of Dr Shiju's interpretation namely the issue of center and the margins defined with the help of the relevant texts.

In our context of pluralism, any discussion on subalternity is significant as the same will present a new direction in terms of the emancipation of the people of the margins. I am sure, this book will initiate a new debate in the field of subaltern hermeneutics in India. I present this book with a real sense of passion and enthusiasm. I hope and pray that Dr Shiju Mathew will be able to systematically write books which will surely enrich the biblical scholarship in India.

Rev. Prof. Dr C. I. David Joy
Principal, KUT Seminary (2019-)
Professor of NT, UTC (1999-2019)
Editorial Board Member of SBL (IVBS) (2017-)

Preface

The present volume is a collection of studies focusing on the theme 'Center and Margin.' With the exception of chapters five and six, and parts of chapter one, all other chapters with some changes are published in Indian and International Journals and in edited books. The journals and edited books in which the other chapters were published are: Ruth, a Moabite Gentile Woman Blessing the Nation Israel: A Subaltern Reading, *NLTJ*, Vol.3, No.2, 2013: 69-77; Law, Land and Gender in the Hebrew Bible: A Postcolonial Womanist Reading, *AJT*, Vol.30, no.2, 2016: 177-192; Affirming the Monotheistic Faith Through Action: Reading the Book of Esther in the Shadow of Persian Imperialism, *UBS Journal.* Vol.12.2, 2018: 35-56; Kingship in Israel: Power Play Behind the Traditions, Vol.8, No.2, 2018: 96-107; Deuteronomy and Women Rights: A Subaltern Reading, in *Journeys into the Deep: Hermeneutical Patterns of M. M. Thomas*, ed. C. I. David Joy and P. Mohan Larbeer, Bangalore: BTESSC, 2016, 53-73 and Ruth: The Immigrant, a Journey from Moab to Bethlehem, *Re-Imagining Reformation: Essays in Honor of P. G. George*, ed. Y. T. Vinayaraj, Dexter Maben and Woba James, Delhi: ISPCK, 2017, 223-237.

The studies are revised and modified to connect it with the central theme 'Center and Margin.' The materials for them are gathered mainly from libraries in Bangalore, Dehradun and Pune.

The book deals with the Biblical Law Codes (Book of the Covenant Code, Holiness Code and the Deuteronomic Code), Kingship in Israel comparing it with Ancient West Asian kingship and Women in the Hebrew Bible.

The projection of the book is to initially bring out the characters of both the Center and the Margin. In Biblical Law Codes, the author brought out selected texts to portray the position of women in all three codes namely the Covenant Code, the Holiness Code and the Deuteronomic Code to project whether it is community of equal or unequal. In the second chapter, the author pointed out that the kingship in ancient Israel was an ill-timed one and was borrowed heavily from the neighboring nations. Since it was not a divinely ordained institution instead of blessings, it fragmented the peace and tranquility of the Israelite society. The powerful dominated the powerless and tradition of center dominated the tradition of margin. The chapter on Ruth, the Outsider and Naomi, the Insider points out how a Moabite woman being a widow changed her social identity of margin among the people of center. The partnering of both the outsider (Ruth) and the insider (Naomi) changed the identity crisis to an identity of respect and honor. The chapter on Esther and Mordecai: The Subalterns focuses how the margin exposed the center using reversal strategy. The passive characters shifted as active characters using banquet strategy. Here also we can see the inside (woman of margin) and outside (man of margin) partnering to foil the plan and strategy of center (Haman). The penultimate chapter is center and margin within the women's world focusing on two characters Sarah and Hagar. Sarah the Center dominated Hagar the Margin. The role of Abraham was passive in nature but God appeared to Hagar and assured the promises of divine presence and blessings of generation similar to Abrahamic promise. In the final chapter, the author brought out the role of margins in delivering and upbringing Moses, the liberator. All women characters took different paths: Midwives took the middle path; Jochebed, the silent but judicious path; Miriam, the wise path; and Pharaoh's daughter, the bold path. All these paths are essential as people of margin to defy the power and order of center.

I thank the Revd. Dr. David Joy, Principal of KUT Seminary and former professor of UTC who has written a foreword to my book. I acknowledge Christian World Imprints, New Delhi for the interest it has shown in publishing my second monograph. The first monograph was *Biblical Law Codes in Creative Tension: A Postcolonial Womanist Reading.*

Shiju Mathew
Associate Professor
HOD (OT) and Dean of PG Studies
UBS, Pune

Chapter 1

Biblical Law Codes: Community of Equal or Unequal

The Covenant Code and the Community

The book of Exodus projects the life of Israel from Egypt 'the place of slavery' to Tabernacle 'the place of worship.' In between these two stages of Israelite life, a series of events took place. These events played and still play a major role in the life of the Church and Society and also serve as a paradigm for the marginalized. The different forms of theology emerged throughout the ages are centered on the liberation experiences of Israel from the hand of the imperial Egypt. The passages such as the story of baby Moses and his miraculous saving from the hand of Pharaoh and the river Nile episode, Israelite walking through the Red Sea on dry land, the wilderness journey, the provision of water and manna brought inspiration throughout the centuries and are the constitutive events for the New Testament believers. But, the legal texts (Exod 20-23) which serves as the connecting link between the salvific event and the settlement period are not given much importance and are left aside and neglected as if they have no bearing to the life and activity of the church and society.

This section is an attempt to help the readers to understand the importance of legal text in addressing the rights of the 'Others,' to ascertain a community of togetherness and belongingness.

The Book of the Covenant Code

The book of Exodus pictures Yahweh as a Liberator. Yahweh comes into the history to liberate the marginalized. The history projecting God as a liberator begins from the book of Exodus. The expression 'bringing forth out of Egypt' (Exod 1-15) is not merely the point of departure but a mighty deed of God as a liberator. The liberation aspect is fourfold: social, economic, political and spiritual. This liberation aspects run throughout the scripture. Old Testament Prophets emphasized the Exodus events to stimulate, challenge and encourage the Israelites to remain faithful and loyal to Yahweh (Isa 43:14-17; Jer 2:2-3; 6:16; Hos 2:14-15; 11:1-4; 12:9; Amos 2:10; 3:1-2; Mic 6:4-5). New Testament too cites the Exodus event to the community of faith to strengthen herself in the midst of struggles and temptation (I Cor. 10:1ff; Gal 5:1; Heb.11:27-29). Moving further to the 20th and 21st century, Liberation theologies like Latin American Theology, Dalit theology, feminist theology and other people centered theologies used the Exodus event as a paradigm to fight for their rights in a power dominated culture and society. Historical critics too considered the Exodus event as the historical and theological starting point of ancient Israel.[1] Hence, the Exodus event is not merely a one-time event happened in the past rather an ongoing experience in the lives of the marginalized communities.

Though the Exodus event in the book of Exodus has highly influenced both the Jewish and the Christian world and is considered as a paradigm for different movements, for instance, the liberation movements, the laws in the same book tends to be more androcentric and not communitarian in nature. The laws related to women seem to be male constructs and sounds as sexist, racist and classist. Hence,

---

[1] Susanne Scholz, "The Complexities of 'His' Liberation Talk: A Literary Feminist Reading of the Book of Exodus," in *Exodus to Deuteronomy*, ed. Athalya Brenner (Sheffield: Sheffield Academic Press, 2000), 21.

a rereading of the law from a margin perspective is essential to ascertain the voice of the voiceless.

The Biblical law codes can be broadly divided into three law codes: (1) The Covenant Code (Ex. 20-23), (2) the Deuteronomic Code (Deut. 12-26) and (3) the Holiness Code (Lev. 17-26). The laws found in the Deuteronomic Code are quite different from that of the Book of the Covenant Code and Holiness Code. The section Exod 20:22-23:19 is a collection of judgments (*Mishpatim*). Unlike the theophany narrative (19:1-20:21), it differs both in form and content. Based on 24:7, this section is known as the Book of the Covenant. The Book of the Covenant has some affinity with the Codes of Mesopotamian civilization such as the code of Hammurabi. The text deals with civil laws such as property, protection rights and theft (Exod 21:1-22:17) and religious, cultic, and moral instruction (Exod 22:18-23:19).

Exodus 20:8-10, 17: Right of Body, Belongings and Liberty

Exodus 20: 8-10: Right for Liberty

The day of rest in Exodus (Exod. 20:8-11) differs from Deuteronomy (Deut 5:12-15). In Exodus, the day of rest is related to creation (v.11) whereas in Deuteronomy the rest is commanded, and the reason for rest is to remember their days of slavery in the land of Egypt (v.15). In Exodus, the seventh day of rest is expected for all members of the community including the aliens (v.10). In Deuteronomy like Exodus, the rest is for all members, but the additional clause 'in order that your male slave and your female slave may rest as well as you' is missing in Exodus (Deut. 5:14; Exod. 20:10). In both texts, the day of rest points not only to a religious observance, but also has a social and humanitarian flavor.

Translation/Textual Comments

8 Remember[2] the Sabbath day to keep it holy[3] 9 Six days you shall labor and do all your work[4] 10 but the seventh day[5] is a Sabbath to the Lord your God; you shall not do[6] any work, you, your son or your daughter, your male[7] or your female slave,[8] or your animals,[9] or the alien in your gates.[10]

The text 20:8-10 is placed outside the Covenant Code. In the Covenant Code, the position of women, slave (male and female) are in a lower status and are in a disadvantaged position, whereas in the Decalogue freedom is given to 'all.

The law of Sabbath commences with the 7th letter of the Hebrew alphabet ָז זָכוֹר and the beneficiaries are not the elite group, rather the whole society. The narrator enlists 7 categories of living beings probably having the number seven (Sabbath) in his mind- you, or your son or your daughter, your male slave or your female slave, your animal or your alien who is in your gate. If we go deeper, the order of creation is of 7 days (cf. Genesis 2:1-3) and the categories

---

[2] The Samaritan Hebrew Pentateuch reads שמור 'keep' c.f. Deut 5:12 (Along with the word 'observe/keep' it also adds a clause 'as YHWH your God commands to you'). The LXX reads 'remember'. In MT, the verb used is זכור 'remember' which is in Qal infinitive absolute (c.f. Exodus 13:3). It is read as an 'emphatic imperative' (legislative command).

[3] *Soph pasuq* is absent in L, but found in number of Manuscripts [see John I. Durham, "Exodus," in *Word Biblical* Commentary, ed. John D. W. Watts and James W. Watts, 3 (USA: Nelson Reference and Electronic, 1987), 277.] לְקַדְּשׁוֹ has preposition ־ל, the infinitive form of the verb.

[4] *Soph Pasuq* is again missing.

[5] The Nash Papyrus and a few manuscripts Septuagint and Vulgate read 'in the seventh day'.

[6] The Nash Papyrus, Septuagint, Syriac and Vulgate add בה for more lucidity as the restriction is applied only on the seventh day.

[7] The Targum and many manuscripts codices minusculis scripti Syriac read 'nor your male slave'. The Parallel version in Deuteronomy also adds w. (Deut. 5:14).

[8] The Nash Papyrus and Septuagint follow Deut. 5:14.

[9] The Samaritan Pentateuch reads 'your animal' and is absent in Targum Pseudo-Jonathan. The Septuagint includes 'your ox and your ass'.

[10] The Septuagint has 'ο παροικων ἐν σοι 'the one residing with you/who dwells with you'. This verse is also without *soph pasuq* in L.

of living beings are 7 and the word starts with the 7th letter of the Hebrew alphabet, which clearly defines the social pattern and are woven into the very fabric of the Israelite society. The Decalogue unlike the Book of the Covenant Code delimits human self-rule and restores human beings irrespective of his/her social standing to a position of freedom. The law promotes human liberty and human equality. The cause of social justice is highly pointed out by issuing the decree and advocating the unchallengeable right of every human being irrespective of his/her societal standing.

Hence, in this law, the whole society irrespective of the standing of each member is given equal opportunity and rights to keep the Sabbath and to partake in it.

Exodus 20:17: Right of Body and Belongings

Translation/Textual Comments

You shall not covet the house of your neighbor.[11] You shall not covet the wife of your neighbor,[12] or his male servant or female servant, or his ox or donkey,[13] or anything that belong to your neighbor.

The exact meaning of לֹא תַחְמֹד (you shall not covet) is a subject of dispute. The word covet means 'wrongful attitude, desire, yearn for, lust after someone or something specifically for one's use or gratification.'[14] According to Wallis, 'the word *chāmadh* refers not to the 'desire' that is inherently human, but the specific act of desire that

[11] Septuagint and the parallel passage in Deuteronomy (5:21) has wife first and house second. The Deuteronomic passage puts wife before house showing the importance of woman in the eyes of law.

[12] Nash Papyrus and few manuscripts Samaritan Pentateuch and Septuagint add 'his field' before 'male servant'. The Deuteronomic passage also has field before male servant (5:21).

[13] Septuagint adds 'or any of his livestock'. It is very interesting to note that the things not to be coveted like 20:8-10 are seven in numbers. The Decalogue starts with 'I am the Lord your God' ends with 'neighbor and his belonging', which clearly points to the importance of neighbor and his belonging in law instituted by God.

[14] John I. Durham, "Exodus," 297. For Scholars' opinion (such as Hyatt and A. Philips) see Durham, "Exodus," 297-298. C.f. Cornelis Houtman, "Exodus," in *Historical Commentary on the Old Testament*, ed. Gert T. M. Prinsloo Cornelis Houtman, Wilfred G. E. Watson and Al Wolters (Leuven: Peeters, 2000), 68-69.

is generated by emotion.[15] Many scholars consider that it connotes practical action, i.e., you shall not do anything in order to acquire what belongs to your neighbour (cf. Exod 34:24; Josh 7:21, Prov 6:25 and Mic 2:2).[16] This word could also be employed as a position of power and unfair rivalry to acquire other's property.[17]

The question here arises is, whether the verb חָמַד points to action like the previous nine commandments, or suggests for desire, or points to both action and desire. If desire, is it possible to put it as a command or legislation? The preceding commandments are full of actions such as 'Do not murder, do not commit adultery, do not steal and do not bear false witness against your neighbour'. Does the tenth commandment (verse 17) go further than the previous commandments pointing that the desire before action is forbidden? There is a possibility as desire for neighbour's property and wife may lead to stealing and adultery. Here, the law clearly forbids the power over others (the possession of neighbour). This perspective is totally missing out in the Covenant Code (cf. Deut 10:17-19, 23:7-8; Lev. 19:13, 17-19).

If we go further by comparing it with the parallel code (Deut 5:21), differences can be seen especially concerning 'wife'. In Deuteronomy, the word תַחְמֹד is used only for wife. The desire for other things is expressed by means of תִתְאַוֶּה. Do these changes refer to sexual desire, stealing or to gain possession of something

---

[15] Hale G. Wallis, "Chāmadh," in *Theological Dictionary of the Old Testament*, ed. G. Johannes Botterweck and Helmer Ringgren (Grand Rapids, Michigan: William B. Eerdmans Publishing Company, 1980), 454. For Wallis, 'the semasiological range of *chāmadh* covers the entire human sequence from viewing through perception of pleasure or even delight and inward longing to the desire to possess…'(454). The word *chāmadh* in the scripture have positive (Psalms 19:10; Prov 21:10), negative (Exod 20:17; Deut 5:21; Josh 7:21), and neutral (Gen 27:15; Psalm 39:11) component (456-457).

[16] U. Cassuto, *A Commentary on the Book of Exodus* (Jerusalem: The Magness Press, 1967), 248. J. Hermann, E. Sellin, Leipzig argues that the verb *hmd* includes the action which stems from the emotion [See Brevard S. Childs, *The Book of Exodus* (London: SCM Press, 1974), 425.] Martin Noth describes this verb as an attempt to attach something to oneself illegally [See Martin Noth, *Exodus* (London: SCM Press, 1962), 166.]

[17] Wallis, "Chāmadh," 459.

that belongs to another? It is difficult to bring out a conclusion. In our observation, in Deuteronomy 'the wife' is highlighted as the main object, and all other, i.e., house, male or female servant, ox and donkey are supplemented, which shows that woman is a full and equal partner of her husband and has rights in society. Unlike Deuteronomy 5:21, in Exodus the place of wife is counted along with male or female servant, ox and donkey. The wife is considered as the property of the husband and is categorized under house 'בֵּית'. The Septuagint version of the Exodus text too supports for Deuteronomistic readings where 'the wife' is mentioned as the main and given a place of her own (*οὐκ ἐπιθυμήσεις τὴν γυναῖκα τοῦ πλησίον σου οὐκ ἐπιθυμήσεις τὴν οἰκίαν τοῦ πλησίον σου οὔτε τὸν ἀγρὸν αὐτοῦ οὔτε τὸν παῖδα αὐτοῦ οὔτε τὴν παιδίσκην αὐτοῦ οὔτε τοῦ βοὸς αὐτοῦ οὔτε τοῦ ὑποζυγίου αὐτοῦ οὔτε παντὸς κτήνους αὐτοῦ οὔτε ὅσα τῷ πλησίον σού ἐστιν*).

Exodus 21:2-11: Laws on Servitude

Translation/Textual Comments

3. When you buy a Hebrew slave, six years he shall serve[18] and in the seventh (year) he shall go out free for nothing. 3. If he will enter in body (single)[19] he shall go out in his body; if husband and wife (married), his wife shall go out with him. 4. If his owner[20] gives to him a wife she bears to him sons or daughters, the wife and her children shall be her[21] master's and he shall go self (alone).[22] 5. But, if

---

[18] The Samaritan Hebrew Pentateuch, Septuagint, Syriac, and Vulgate adds a pronominal suffix 'you'.

[19] Samaritan Pentateuch reads *in his back or self.* The word בְּגַפּוֹ literally means 'with his body', i.e., alone. The Septuagint translates it as 'If he comes in single' (ἐὰν αὐτὸς μόνος εἰσέλθῃ).

[20] Septuagint, Syriac, and Vulgate read *his master.*

[21] Samaritan, Textus Graecus Originalis (Septuagint), Syriac, and Vulgate reads *his.*

[22] Or in his back or self.

the slave plainly says,[23] I love my master, my wife, and my children;[24] I will not go out free, 6. then his master shall draw near him to God;[25] and he shall draw (bring) him to door or the door post; and his master shall pierce his ear through an awl; and he shall serve him forever. 7. When a man sells his daughter as a maidservant, she shall not go out as the male slaves go forth. 8. If she does not please her master, who has appointed her for himself,[26] then he shall let her be redeemed; he shall have no right to sell her to a foreigner, since he has dealt deceitfully (unfaithfully) with her. 9. If he betrothed her for his son, he shall do justice to her as his daughter. 10. If he takes another wife to himself, he shall not diminish (restrain) her food, her clothing or her marital rights. 11. And if he does not do these three (things) for her, she shall go out freely (for nothing), without money.

Comments and Explanation

Exodus 21:2-11 deals with the treatment of the slaves within Israel, most probably native slaves. It is introduced by *when,* but the lesser clauses are introduced by *if.* In this passage, the problem to be addressed first is what is meant by the phrase עֶבֶד עִבְרִי (Hebrew Slave)? This phrase is debatable and grammatically can be understood in different ways. It can mean either a Hebrew (man) servant or (man) servant of a Hebrew.[27] In the latter case the servant can be either a Hebrew or a foreigner. If we compare the parallel law in Deuteronomy 15:12, the slave is a Hebrew. The question arises now is: who is an עִבְרִי (Hebrew)? עִבְרִי has a very distinctive significance. It has been taken both as a designation of a *native* slave, an Israelite slave, and also an underprivileged social group, disadvantaged persons who fall

---

[23] The Hebrew word וְאִם־אָמֹר יֹאמַר is emphatic.

[24] In verse 4, for Children ילדים is used, whereas in verse 5, בתי is indicated. There is no specific and clear reason for a change.

[25] Septuagint reads *to the God's judgment.*

[26] Samaritan adds *to him.*

[27] William H. C. Propp, *Exodus 19-40,* in *The Anchor Bible,* ed. William Foxwell Albright and David Noel Freedman (New York: Doubleday, 2006), 186-187.

easily into the oppression of slavery.[28] For centuries, the term עִבְרִי has been associated with a Jew. The table of the nations in Gen 10:24-25 include an individual named Eber which is also pronounced as עֵבֶר. Does this name עֵבֶר refers to all the עִבְרִים? If so, it refers not only to the people of Israel but also to all Eber's sons which include the Arameans, Moabites, Ammonites, and Edomites etc. Interestingly, Abram is addressed as Hebrew (Gen 14:13). If so, it refers to the descendants of Abram.[29] Recent study has made it clear that the term does not designate an ethnic/racial group, but rather a pejorative designation of a legal or social status within the Ancient West Asian society of the second millennium BCE (who became slaves). The Hebrew were the disadvantaged peoples, considered inferior, having more or less no rights in the society, and were employed in the menial laboring jobs.[30] So, Hebrew is not necessarily ethnic but probably a depressed social class.

The term עִבְרִי is mentioned in the scripture in two contexts: a) in the mouth of foreigners; b) describing slaves. Whatever their nationality is, they were slaves with a certain hope of freedom after a set term of servitude. So, they can't be categorized as full citizens, or as full slaves. At the end of six years, whatever the cause of servitude is,

---

[28] Durham, "Exodus," 320. The general consensus among the scholars (M. Greenberg, B. S. Childs and others) is that the term Hebrew is not an ethnic term but a disadvantaged social group within the Ancient West Asian society of the second millennium BCE. They were the landless people who were dependent on wealthy people for survival. For von Rad, from a sociological point of view they were the fluctuating element of the population and from legal and economic point of view a lower class [Gerhard von Rad, *Deuteronomy*, (London: SCM Press, 1966) 107.] c.f. Anthony Philips, "The Laws of Slavery: Exodus 21:2-11," *JSOT* 30 (1984): 51-66.; N. P. Lemche, "The Hebrew Slave: Comments on the Slave Law Exodus 21:2-11," *Vetus Testamentum* 25 (1975): 129-144.; Noth, *Exodus*, 177. and G. Henton Davies, *Exodus* (London: SCM Press Ltd, 1967), 175.

[29] Propp, "Exodus 19-40," 186. The term עִבְרִי can also mean 'the one from across'. From a Palestinian perspective, עִבְרִי denotes 'Easterner'. Canaan was included in the region 'across the river'. It also connotes a 'westerner' which refers to the Amorite (c.f. 186).

[30] Childs, *The Book of Exodus*, 468.

עִבְרִי was free[31] to go. For Alan Cole, the slave mentioned in the text is an indentured laborer bound for six years, and when his seventh year comes to an end, he must be released.[32] The time bond of the slaves is varied. The slaves of Nuzi were apparently slaves for life, though there is a different view. The Torah, on the other hand, enacts that the Hebrew slave shall serve only a limited time, and thereafter he shall be free. In the Hammurabi Code (§117), a fixed period of three years is laid down only in the case where a Babylonian freeman sells himself, his wife, or his son, or his daughter on account of debts.[33]

The next issue to be addressed is whether the word Hebrew refers to male members only or refers also to female? Septuagint text reads, *Ἐὰν κτήσῃ παῖδα Εβραῖον*. 'If you buy a Hebrew servant.' The Masoretic text refers Hebrew as masculine, but both Deuteronomy and Septuagint mentions it in a generic case.[34] If so, it can't be claimed as exclusively male slave or female slave. It can be either or both. If both, why the MT says, six years *he* shall serve you? What about *she*? Going further, the law states that *the male slave shall go out free, without debt.*[35] The provision aspect is missing in

---

[31] The term *free* is another disputed term. It designates apparently a social status free of bondage, but somewhat below the category of free citizen. It also seems to denote a definite class in society lying between nobles and slaves. Hence, it is a social term indicating a status higher than slavery, but below a full free Israelite.

[32] Alan Cole, *Exodus: An Introduction and Commentary* (England: Inter-Varsity Press, 1973), 165.

[33] Cassuto, *A Commentary on the Book of Exodus*, 266. See also J. P. Hyatt, *Exodus* (London: Oliphants, 1971), 228. The Law in Exodus 21:2-6 has its parallel in § 117 of the Hammurabi Code. Lemche and a good number of scholars consider that the laws of slavery has strong connection to Canaanite and Mesopotamian Laws (c.f. N P Lemche, "Manumission of Slaves-the Fallow Year-the Sabbatical Year-the Jubilee Year," *Vetus Testamentum* 26, no. 1 (1976).)

[34] See F. Wilbur Gingrich, William F. Arndy *A Greek-English Lexicon of the New Testament and Other Early Christian Literature* (Chicago: The University of Chicago Press, 1957), 609. παῖδα can be used with reference to a relation between one human being and another, and ον ending in Εβραῖον can be used sometimes for feminine.

[35] The Code of Hammurabi (§117) says, 'if a man gives his wife, son, or daughter as a slave to work off a debt, they may do this for three years, but shall be free in the fourth'.

this passage, which differs from the parallel Deuteronomic passage. Deuteronomy 15:12 requires that the owner shall not send the slave empty-handed. He has to provide him liberally (economically) so that the slave may not again turn to slavery. The law further says, if he enters his owner's house with his wife, his wife can go out along with him. The woman is mentioned as the wife of the enslaved man. But, if his master gives him a wife and if she bears him children, he can go free, but his wife and children belongs to his master.[36] It brings out a clear picture that the slaves are treated by the owner not as human being, but rather as a property. This also clearly indicates the freedom from bondage, but not as a full citizen. It is an act of inducement to renounce his right of freedom after six years of faithful service. It also contradicts with Gen. 2:24, 'therefore shall a man leave his father and mother, and shall cleave unto his wife, and they shall be one flesh'. The temporary slave who does not want to be separated from his wife and children will opt for servitude forever, and will swear an oath of loyalty to his owner. How can the law (Exod 21:3-4) contradict with the commandment of God? The slave woman also is not given the freedom of choice. The wife mentioned here is presumably a perpetual slave, and therefore the master's own property. Some consider it as a Neolithic matriarchal society here, with the relationship to mother closer than that to the father.[37] Here at least the husband has the provision to stay with his wife and children, or to go alone. The wife can be either the property

---

[36] In the Ancient West Asia, it was a common practice for an owner to force or allow a slave to have children from a foreign female slave. It was solely for the purpose of adding house born slaves. The woman and her offspring remained his property. Ur-Namma 4 says 'If a male slave marries a female slave, and that male slave is later given freedom, she/he will not leave the home'. It reflects the very attitude of treating slaves as property rather than persons. In the text, the wife given to a slave is probably a freeborn Hebrew slave who was sold by her father. The Late-Bronze Age site of Emar 16 in Syria treats the issue of what to do when a man, in servitude receives a wife from his master and then leaves the household (c.f. Bruce Wells, "What Is Biblical Law? A Look at Pentateuchal Rules and near Eastern Practice," *The Catholic Biblical* Quarterly 70 (2008); 233-234).

[37] Cole, *Exodus:An Introduction and Commentary,* 165-166. The traditional Jewish view traces ethnic identity through mother, whereas all biblical evidence suggests that in Israelite time ethnic identity passed through father.

of her slave husband or master husband. The law seems to be not in favor of freedom for female slave.

But if the slave plainly says-Is this statement made by the slave induced by slave's free will decision or part of the legal formula? Is the declaration made by the slave meant that his love to his master is out of sheer faithfulness or fear? Does his love towards his master coincide with his love towards his wife and children? The text is not spelling out clearly. Most probably the slave fears for an impoverished state, which may perhaps lead to servitude as he would seldom have enough resources to establish himself as a free citizen and to take care of his family. So, out of fear and circumstantial compulsion he may have made such a statement.

Moving further to vv. 7-11, the structure of verse 7 is different from verse 2. In verse 2 the buyer is the subject whereas in verse 7, the slave is the subject, i.e., the girl's father is the subject. The parallel passage in Deut.15:12 emphasize a generous and liberal approach towards both the Hebrew male and female. In Exodus, the female is placed under male, and is treated as a property that can change hands from one owner to another, whereas in Deuteronomy both male and female are considered as equal partners having same rights. In the Covenant Code, the freedom is granted for male slave after the completion of six years but this rule is not applied for female slave. 'She shall not go out as the male slaves do' clearly indicates that unlike male slave, female slave is enslaved for life. The male slaves are having the right to leave after six years and if they are willing can be as slaves for life. In the case of female, there is no provision of release after six years. It appears that the daughters are solely the property of fathers or husbands. It also ensures that the daughter may never leave male control, which shows male supremacy.[38] It contradicts with the parallel law found in Deuteronomy 15:12-18.

So, in this section (vv. 7-11), female slave is categorized in a different way as compared to that of the male slave. The rules for the male slave and female slave are opposed to each other. She can't go free after six years (cf. Deut 15:12-15) because her master-husband

[38] Drorah O' Donnel Setel, 'Exodus', in *Women's Bible Commentary*, ed. Carol A. Newsom and Sharon H. Ringe (Kentucky: John Knox Press, 1998), 38.

still has duties towards her. So, the expectation of seventh-year release was denied to women. Unlike men, women do not enjoy full social equality, as they are regarded as property. The code here puts men as the one who rules over the enslaved women. In other words, they are slaves for life. In Deut. 15:12, both the man and the woman are accorded the right of freedom in the seventh year. Exodus 21:7 says, when a man sells his daughter as a slave, she shall not go out as the male slaves do. Now, we must keep in mind, the reason behind for selling a girl. It might be poverty, debt, etc. It is the same case with male slaves also. Then, why there is discrimination between male and female?

Exodus 21:22-27: The Laws on Ill-Treatment towards the 'Others'

Translation/Textual Comments

20 If a man strikes his male slave or female slave with a rod[39] and the slave dies on the spot,[40] he shall be punished.[41] 21 But if the slave survives a day or two, he shall not be punished,[42] for he is his property.[43]

22 If men fight[44] and they hit a pregnant woman and she has a premature birth of her children[45] but there is no further injury,[46]

---

[39] Samaritan Pentateuch omits 'with a rod'.

[40] Slave dies immediately.

[41] Samaritan Pentateuch has 'he shall be put to death'.

[42] Samaritan Pentateuch reads 'to be put to death' i.e. he shall not be put to death.

[43] Or for the slave is his property or his money.

[44] Or if men who are fighting injure a pregnant woman. The verb *ngp* implies malicious, hostile and deliberate act [Stanley Isser, "Two Traditions: The Law of Exodus 21:22-23 Revisited," *The Catholic Biblical Quarterly* 52 (1990), 39].

[45] Samaritan Pentateuch and Septuagint read 'and her child go/come out'. Birth as a result of accidental hit is mentioned in this text. It is not clear why the phrase expressing the premature birth speaks of children in plural.

[46] The Palestinian reading in Jewish tradition interprets אָסוֹן as damage or harm, even death (cf. Gen. 42:4, 38; 44:29). BDB gives 'mischief, evil, harm'. In this text, it refers to a fatal injury in addition to the miscarriage. Targum Onqelos and Vulgate translate אָסוֹן as death. The LXX version relates the injury not to the

the one who is responsible shall be fined[47] whatever the woman's husband demands and the Judge determines. 23 But, if there is further injury then you are to take life for life,[48] 24 eye for eye, tooth for tooth, hand for hand, foot for foot, 25 burn for burn,[49] wound for wound, stripe for stripe.

26 And if man hits the eyes of his male slave or eyes of his female slave, and destroys it, he shall let the slave go free because of the eyes. 27 If he knocks out the tooth of a male slave or female slave, he shall let the slave go free because of the tooth.

Comments and Explanation

The ill-treatment done towards the slave is not prohibited in the laws. The striking of the slave is projected as a normal practice. The action will be taken only, if the slave dies. The nature and quantum of punishment is not clearly stated and is vague. The Samaritan text justifies by the judgment 'he shall be put to death'. The slaves like the free are created in His image and whoever attacks shall be punished by the law. However, in this text the victim's case is not justified.[50] The treatment towards a slave is a discouraging one. In Verse 12, a man who kills a man is put to death. But if a man kills a slave, he is only punished. The slave is of less value and is considered as a property.

The law is lenient towards the owner. The text is not clear in making the judgment 'but if the slave survives a day or two'. The

---

mother but to the foetus. However, among the scholars there are mixed opinions. Some argue for foetus and others argues for mother (c.f. Isser: 30-33).

[47] The LXX version reads singular instead of Plural 'If two men fight and strike...., he shall be fined.....'

[48] Does life for life refer to the life of the wife of the offender? (CH § 210). If this opinion is considered favourably, the sufferer/loser is woman.

[49] Samaritan Pentateuch has 'burn-spot, scar of a burn' instead of 'burning'.

[50] The Jewish interpreters Rashi, B. Jacob and U. Cassuto defend the view by stating that a death penalty is intended in the phrase 'he shall surely be punished'. The Talmud (San. 52b) orders for execution and that too by beheading for such a crime. [c.f. Childs, 471.] The text however, doesn't stand in line with the opinion of the Jewish interpreters and Talmud. The view negating death can be supported with the following verse '...because he is his property.

possibility of death is placed in favor of the owner assuming that the death occurred not by the beating of the owner but rather due to some other reason. The law is safeguarding the owner by giving him the benefit of doubt. For R. E. Clements, the benefit of doubt is given to the owner as it is assumed that he would not purposefully destroy his own property.[51] In this text, the law is safeguarding the powerful and justice is not given to the weak. The accuser has been let off with an understanding that he has already received punishment through the loss of his property.

Does this expression mean that the owner has the rights to beat the slave? Was it due to the imperial values practiced by the Israelite society? The Book of the Covenant legitimizes the slavery and its societal structure. It promotes slavery by supporting the rights of the master by discriminating the slaves.[52] The position of slave as his master's property is not a practice found only in Israel, rather a common practice throughout Ancient West Asia. This imperialistic tendency practiced by the powerful nations got influenced in the social life of Israel.

The law stated in Exodus 21:22-25 consists of protasis and apodosis. The protasis describes the striking of a pregnant woman resulting into miscarriage and the apodosis prescribes the consequences, i.e., the duty of the accused to pay for the damages. An androcentric view can be seen in this passage, where the husband and the judge determine the compensation. There are mixed opinion among the scholars concerning the injury of a pregnant woman who was inflicted in a fight. Usually it is understood as an accident, but scholars like D. Daube[53] argued for an act of malevolent intent. Daube argues that the words 'he shall pay as the judges determine' are a later addition, and it was added to limit the power of the victim's husband.[54] The precise amount is not specified. The amount is fixed

---

[51] Ronald E. Clements, *Exodus* (Cambridge: Cambridge University Press, 1972), 138.

[52] Cole, *Exodus: An Introduction and Commentary*, 169.

[53] D. Daube, *Studies in Biblical Law* (Cambridge: Cambridge University Press, 1947), 100.

[54] Daube, *Studies in Biblical Law,* 108.

by the woman's husband and is subjected to the final verdict of the judges. The practice of fine is common to the Ancient West Asian law. The pain and suffering meted out by the woman is not considered, as it is assumed that she got injured due to her intervention in the fighting between men. The amount is decided by the male members of the community. The law says, '*Whatever the woman's husband...*' This inexact edict is surprising, as it is difficult to ascertain whether the injury caused to woman was an accidental or a deliberate act. In either case, the compensation is decided by her husband and the judge. It appears that the judge is purposefully placed to make certain that the money demanded by the victim's husband be justifiable. It also brings out a clear picture that the victim being a woman has no voice and the decision makers are her husband and the judge, rulers of the household and society. It points out that 'the women's bodies were not merely controlled but actually owned.'[55]

Exodus 22:16-17 (Eng.) [15-16 Heb.]:"[56] Virgin as Property

Translation/Textual Comments

16 If a man seduces[57] a virgin who is not betrothed[58] and lies with her, he shall pay the bride price for her and make her his wife.17 If[59] her father absolutely/utterly refuses to give her to him, he shall pay money[60] equivalent to the bride price for virgins.

[55] Setel, 'Exodus,' 38.

[56] Alexander Rofe argues that this law like 21:22-25 did not originally belong to the Covenant Code but was added to the collection at a later stage [see Alexander Rofe, 'Deuteronomy: Issues and Interpretations' in *Old Testament Studies*, ed. David J. Reimer (London: T&T Clark, 2002), 172].

[57] By persuasion or by deception but not by coercion.

[58] Betrothal was very important in Israelite life and was the first stage of the marriage. Important decisions regarding finance take place during this occasion. The betrothal girl comes almost under the category of married woman and the laws are same for both. Here the text means that she had never been betrothed for if the *mohar* was paid, the girl was considered *me'orasah* (betrothed).

[59] Few manuscripts such as Samaritan, Septuagint and Syriac version prefer a conjunction 'And/But'.

[60] Septuagint translates it as 'to pay restitution to the father' (ἀποτείσει τῷ πατρὶ).

Comments and Explanation

This section comes under the heading "social and religious law". The Book of the Covenant unlike Deuteronomy does not contain a section dealing with marriage laws (Deut. 22:13-26). The law stated here is about the seduction of a girl who is not betrothed and is placed under property laws. The intention behind the law is not the rights of the girl or the purity of the marriage rather the amount of compensation.[61] The text is about the law of the seducer. A man has seduced a virgin who is not betrothed. A virgin was considered her father's property and he would receive for her the bride price (*mohar*)[62] customarily paid by the husband-to-be. This amount is against the loss of the daughter's services and potential value to the family (cf. Deut 22:13-19; Lev. 21:13-15).[63] By the loss of her virginity, she lost her social status and her value. Her father, as a result has the right to claim for compensation. It underscores that 'the virginity was not ethical rather economic.'[64] For Anderson, 'the rape of an unmarried female injured her father rather than the female herself, which clearly points out that the law do not take into account the female's perspective.'[65]

The seduction by a man is treated as adultery and the punishment for such a crime is death (Deut. 22:23-27). Unlike Deuteronomic passage, the punishment for the man in this text is

---

[61] G. Henton Davies, *Exodus* (London: SCM Press, 1967), 183. Ibn Ezra points out that the sequence of legal topics is from the case of a 'stolen property' to a 'stolen heart'. Both are crimes that result into economic losses and entail compensation [See Nahum M Sarna, "Exodus," in *The Jerusalem Publication Society Torah* Commentary, ed. Nahum M. Sarna (Jerusalem: The Jewish Publication Society, 1991), 134].

[62] The origin of the term *mohar* is uncertain. Since it is common to Hebrew, Ugaritic, Aramaic and Arabic, the practice must have been widespread (Cf. Genesis 34). The *mohar* in other part of the Old Testament was paid in services or heroic deeds (Gen 29:15-20, 27-28; Josh 15:16-17; Judg 1:12-13; I Sam 17:25; 18:20-27; II Sam 3:14). C.f. Sarna, "Exodus," 135.

[63] Sarna, "Exodus," 134.

[64] Setel, "Exodus," 39.

[65] Cherly B. Anderson, *Ancient Laws and Contemporary Controversies* (Oxford: Oxford University Press, 2009), 4, 32-33.

to pay the bride-price and to accept her as his wife, provided her father agrees to it. The choice to give her daughter is the prerogative of the father. If not, still he has to pay the bride-price. In either way, the woman has no rights to express her opinion and she does not participate in the legal course of action. The text is not clear in stating, if the father accepts the seducer and the woman dislikes him. The seduction of a virgin by a man concerns only her father and the seducer. The upper hand on the whole issue lies in the male member of the society and the receiving end is the woman. The androcentric approach can't be negated in this law.[66]

So, the law provides two options and both to victim's father. Either he can demand the bride price and ask him to marry or he may refuse to give his daughter and demand the bride-price for a virgin. The acceptance and refusal are under the control of victim's father. The law restricts the voice of the victim.

Exodus 23:12, 17: Laws on Sabbath, Annual Festivals and the 'others'

Translation/Textual Comments

12 Six days you shall do your works but on the seventh day you are to rest in order that your ox and your donkey may rest and the son of your female servant[67] and the alien may be refreshed/take breathe.[68]

---

[66] The Law resembles with Middle Assyrian Laws, where the victims are either the virgin who was ravished by the seducer or the wife of the seducer. MAL §§ 55-56- If a man takes the virgin by force and seduces her........the father of the virgin shall take the wife of the virgin's seducer and give her to be seduced... the father could then give his daughter in marriage to the seducer. But if he is not having wife, the father can ask the seducer to pay third in silver to her father as the value of a virgin (and) her seducer shall marry her and not cast her off. If the father does not wish, he shall receive the third for the virgin in silver and give his daughter to whom he wishes. If the virgin has given herself to the man, the man shall swear and they shall not touch his wife; the seducer shall give the third in silver as the value of the virgin and the father shall treat his daughter as he wishes. The third in silver is interpreted by some as threefold of the usual amount and others consider it as one-third of the amount.

[67] Samaritan Pentateuch reads it differently: 'your male slave and your female slave like yourself and all your animals'.

[68] The verb is in Niphal imperfect- 'to take a break or be refreshed.'

17 Three times in the year all of your males shall appear before the face of the Lord God.[69]

Comments and Explanation

Verse 12: It seems verse 12 is incomplete. The phrase 'the son of your female servant' is problematic as it indicates the son of female servant and misses out the daughter/s of female servant. The Samaritan Pentateuch reads it as 'male and female slave' instead of 'the son of female slave'. The Samaritan Pentateuch version seems to be more genuine and reasonable comparing it with 20:8-10 and other passages.

In verse 17, the male has been given the rights and privilege to appear before the presence of the Lord, which is a clearly androcentric in nature. The rights and privileges of female are missing. The story of Hannah in I Samuel 1-2 presents a clear picture that women were permitted to enter the temple and had access to make the pilgrimage. Deuteronomy 16:11, 14 include daughter, female slave and strangers among those who are to appear before the Lord.[70]

Summary

The pertinent question to be addressed is: If the Covenant Code comes right after the great salvific event, why the laws are not in favor of all? Whether the final shaping of the Book of the Covenant Code took place in the later period of Israelite history. This view can't be negated as all laws are subjected to change. The book of the covenant code reached to its present form in 8th century BCE. The Assyrian Empire which was strong during the reign of Assurbanipal and Shalmaneser III (9th century BCE) became weak between 783 and 745 BCE. Both Israel and Judah became strong during the reigns of Jeroboam II in Israel and Uzziah of Judah. During this period both Israel and Judah underwent great socio-political changes. Probably they were influenced by the presence of Assyria and other neighboring nations. In order to maintain the economic

---

[69] Septuagint, Syriac and Vulgate reads it as 'the Lord your God'. Samaritan Pentateuch reads 'ark' instead of 'Lord' (c.f. Exodus 34:24).

[70] Sarna, "Exodus," 146.

and political position, lot of changes were made. The gap between the rich and the poor increased. These changes can be seen in the covenant code.

If we compare the Covenant Code with the other two codes Deuteronomic and Holiness Code, the covenant code is patriarchal and colonial in nature. The laws are either apodictic or casuistic in style. The apodictic laws are generally addressed through the male members and are patriarchal in approach whereas the casuistic laws are both patriarchal and colonial. The casuistic laws can be seen throughout the Ancient West Asian laws. They portray a man's world where women are merely a class of property. The full membership is limited to the male members of the society (Exod 20:17; 21:7-11). The sexuality of woman was regarded as the exclusive property of the male members of the society. For e.g., having illicit affairs with a married woman was treated as serious crime, not because of the demoralizing and dehumanizing effect on the victim, but as violation against her husband (Exod 20:14, 17; Lev 20). Having forceful extramarital sex with an unmarried girl by a male member can be legally compensated by marrying that girl in marriage and payment of *mohar* (gift) to the parents. This laws stand in conflict with the liberative experience of Israel where all members experienced God's saving action and freedom in their life. In short, the casuistic laws are more oppressive and repressive in nature, where the powerful dominate the powerless. The voice and rights of women are denied due to androcentric politics. The apodictic laws unlike the casuistic laws though patrirachal are rather egalitarian in nature and the liberating aspect can be seen, which is in line with the Israel's unique history of liberation.

The primary intention of the Covenant law was to treat and take care of those who were in need irrespective of their class and color but over a period of time, most probably the influence of Ancient West Asia (Code of Hammurabi and the Middle Assyrian laws in particular) changed the real essence of the Covenant Code. The laws which we are having now appear to be a modified one. The Covenant Code especially the casuistic laws related to women are colonial in color as it resembles with the laws of the neighboring nations. The laws on dowry, marriage, covetousness, adultery and slavery are unfavorable to women. Discrimination against women is seen both in socio-political and religious sphere which results in disability and impingement on women's lives. Hence, the laws, which appear to be pro-colonial in color, needs to be deconstructed and more inclusive and life affirming laws are needed which can make the foundations of our society strong. It is important for women to break out from the norms and traditional shackles and actively engage themselves in every activity by experimenting with life. The weaker sections especially the women must claim back the position that they have lost by looking at the biblical laws with a new eyes.

The Holiness Code and the Community

God is Holy and the Covenant people are expected to be holy. Holiness is measured not merely based on observance of rituals or adhering to the prescribed set of rules rather grounded on healthy relationship with both fellow human being and the creator God. Breaking of this relationship leads to division and exile. This can be seen in the life of the people of Israel. Messages of disobedience and the consequent downfall reverberate throughout the prophetical books. The departure from right relationship resulted into a fragmented and confused state ensuing into disintegrated society/ nation. In order to ensure harmonious and healthy relationship, rules/norms were set up. But, the sad reality is that the people in the center dictate and stipulates the terms and conditions to those who are in the periphery. The pertinent question that comes to the mind of the reader is: how to take the law as a measuring rod to advocate for the rights of the marginalia?

This section is an attempt to read the laws of Holiness Code from margin perspective to ascertain the rights and voices of the people who are in the periphery.

The Holiness Code

The laws in Leviticus (17) 18-26 are distinctively substantiated by Yahweh's self-introduction 'I am Holy.' The holiness aspect is given prime importance in this set of laws. Due to this characteristic, Klostermann in 1877 named this corpus *Das Heiligkeitsgesetz*, "the

Holiness Code."[71] And from then on, this name continued to have been referred to this section as Holiness Code.

The Nature of Holiness Code

There are differences of opinion regarding the nature of Holiness Code. For Gordon J. Wenham, cleanness is the natural state of most creatures. Holiness is a state of grace to which 'men/women' are called by God, and it is attained through obeying the law and carrying out rituals such as sacrifice. Uncleanness is a substandard condition to which 'men/women' descend through bodily processes and sin. Every Israelite had a duty to seek release from the uncleanness through washing and sacrifice, because uncleanness was quite incompatible with the holiness of the Covenant people."[72] But, Mary Douglas, the feminist theologian goes beyond Wenham. For her, holiness is not merely an act of separation, rather it means more than separation to divine service. It means wholeness and completeness. She quotes Lev. 21:17-21, listing imperfections that block one from acting as a priest, and puts forward in nutshell as, 'He must be perfect as a 'man', if he is to be a priest.'[73] So, for her, holiness is exemplified by completeness. It requires that individuals should conform to the class to which they belong, and it requires that different classes of things shall not be confused. The idea of wholeness or normality as the notion implicitly assumed to be essential to holiness and cleanness is the key for determining the divisions of the animal kingdom.[74] For Wenham, holiness is something given by God and human being can achieve it by obeying the law, and it can be done through sacrifice. But, for Douglas, it is not limited only for divine service; rather it has to do with wholeness and completeness.

Taking these two schools of thought into consideration, we can arrive at a possible conclusion that Holiness is not merely based on

[71] John E. Hartley, "Leviticus," in *Word Biblical Commentary*, ed. John D. W. Watts, 4 (Texas: Word Books, 1992), 247-248.

[72] Gordon J. Wenham, "The Book of Leviticus," in *The New International Commentary on the Old Testament*, ed. R. K. Harrison (Grand Rapids, Michigan: William B. Eerdmans Publishing Company, 1979), 23.

[73] Mary Douglas, *Purity and Danger* (London: Routledge, 1966), 51.

[74] Mary Douglas, *Purity and Danger*, 53.

adhering to a set of rituals and regulations but also to bring wholeness and completeness. This wholeness and completeness can be achieved by considering the dignity of all and giving space to the 'others.' Almost all OT prophets air the view that 'morality/ethics' should go hand in hand with 'religion.'

Reading the Laws through the eyes of the Margin

Though the Law of Holiness is from chapter 17 through 26, the two texts on cleanness regulations (Lev.12:1-8 and 15:16-31) are added in our study as it deals with women who comes under the category of margins. The study of these two texts will also help us to know, how it differs from the laws of Holiness Code.

Leviticus 12:1-8 - Laws on Ritual Purity of a Woman who has given Birth

The book of Leviticus contains a series of regulations and laws. The major part of the book deals with laws on ritual purity (11-15), holy living (17-26), and tithes and offerings (27-34). The section (Lev. 11-15) contains a series of laws that emphasize on ritual purity, i.e., clean and unclean, whereas the section 17-26 deals about holy living, i.e., holy and common. In between these two sections, the regulation for the Day of Atonement is stated (Lev. 16). In short, ritual purity leads to holy living through atonement.

Though the first two texts selected for the study, i.e., Leviticus 12:1-8 and 15:16-31 come under the section on ritual purity (Priestly Code) and are outside the Holiness code [(17)18-26], they are interconnected[75] and also associated with and literally connected

[75] The Priestly Code like Holiness Code was compiled almost at the same time (exilic or early post exilic period). It is assumed that the Priestly writer or a final redactor would have incorporated the Holiness code as both had almost same theological stance. See Chilkuri Vasantha Rao, *Ecological and Theological Aspects of Some Animal Laws in the Pentateuch* (Delhi: ISPCK, 2005), 39-40. For Hartley, there is an interconnection from chapter 11 through 26. Chapters 11-15 deal on the state of uncleanness, chapter 16 is a regulation for the Day of Atonement that removes the state of uncleanness, and chapters 17-26 set forth series of ethical integrity and cultic purity, a forgiven community has to follow.

with the cause of women. The author strongly feels to have it along with the texts on Holiness code.

Translation/Textual Comments

1 The Lord spoke to Moses[76] saying, 2 say to the sons of Israel, saying, when a woman conceives[77] and bears a male child, she shall be ceremonially unclean seven days, as the days of her monthly period, she shall be unclean. 3 On the eighth day, the flesh of his foreskin shall be circumcised.[78] 4 Then she shall wait (remain) thirty three days in the blood of her purifying; she shall not touch any holy thing, or come into the sanctuary until the days of her purifying are completed. 5 But if she bears a female child, then she will be unclean two weeks, as in her period; and she shall wait sixty-six days in the blood of her purifying. 6 And when the days of her purifying are over, whether for a son or a daughter, she shall bring to the priest at the door of the tent of meeting a lamb a year old[79] for a burnt offering, and a young pigeon or turtledove for a sin offering. 7 And he shall offer it[80] before the Lord, and make atonement for her,[81] and then she shall be clean[82] from her flow of blood. This is the law for her who bears a child, male or female. 8 But, if she cannot afford a

---

[76] The absence of Aaron's name in the introductory formula is striking (cf. Lev. 11:1, 13:1; 15:1) since it deals with ritual purity.

[77] תַזְרִיעַ - Literally, the word means 'produce/sow seed'. The Samaritan Hebrew Pentateuch and Septuagint have a niphal form 'to become pregnant, to conceive' whereas MT uses hiphil form (c.f. Gen 1:11-12 'plants bearing seed'). The hiphil form is used probably to emphasize the procedure 'to conceive a child (Produces offspring)' [c.f. Walter C. Kaiser, "The Book of Leviticus," in *The New Interpreter's Bible*, ed. Leander E. Keck (Nashville: Abingdon Press, 1994), 1085].

[78] The Samaritan Hebrew Pentateuch adds את, the sign of the definite direct object. The MT is in Niphal imperfect form 'he is to be circumcised'.

[79] Lit., Son of his year (cf. Exodus 12:5; 29:38; Lev. 23:12, 18, 19; Num 6:12, 14; 7:15, 17, 21, 23, 29).

[80] The expression 'it' refers to both burnt offering and sin offering.

[81] The Hebrew manuscripts, Samaritan Hebrew Pentateuch, Septuagint, Syriac and Targum pseudo-Jonathae add הַכֹּהֵן 'the priest' (cf. v. 8).

[82] The Septuagint has και καθαριει΄αυτῆν 'and it cleanses her'.

lamb, then she shall bring two turtledoves or two young pigeons,[83] one for a burnt offering and the other for a sin offering; and the priest shall make atonement for her, and she shall be clean.

Comments and Explanation

The law in chapter 12[84] defines the ritual status of an Israelite mother (cultic uncleanness) following the child birth. The reason for such purification is not specified in the text. The text makes a distinction between the birth of a male child (vv. 2-4) and a female child (v. 5). The period of uncleanness for a female child and the time period for a mother to keep herself away from holy activities is double than that of a male child. The text is not stating the reason for such a distinction. After stating the distinction between the male and female child, the law adds an instruction about the offerings to be brought to the priest for cleansing, which is same both for a male and female child (vv. 6-7). Verse 8 deals with a provision if she is poor and cannot afford a lamb.

The sexual activities and childbirth were understood as unclean. The reason for such understanding is because of some mysterious powers and activities.[85] This belief is known throughout Ancient West Asia. Does Israel inclined to such a belief? If marriage is ordained by God (Genesis 2), why sexual activity and childbirth are considered as 'unclean'? Why must the woman only enact a purification ritual when she has not sinned? The creator had told the human being to 'Be fruitful and multiply, and fill the earth', then why should a woman be considered unclean when she obeys and follows the command of God.[86] How can the given text contradict with the command of God? We cannot any longer know the reason for such changes in the custom as the text has not specified here or anywhere else.

---

[83] The Samaritan reverses the order of these sacrifices.

[84] Chapter 12 and 15 deal with the impurities female incur in giving birth and genital discharges both male and female incur respectively.

[85] Martin Noth, *Leviticus* (Philadelphia: Westminstress Press, 1965), 97.

[86] Wenham, "The Book of Leviticus,"187.

The issue here is not only to know how this practice of discriminating against women came into Israel, rather why distinction is made between male and female child. Why only mother has to appear before the priest for offering and not her husband? The text is not specifying clearly. Throughout Ancient West Asia, there is a belief that the birth of a female child was more dangerous for the mother than that of a male child, and they also consider that hostile supernatural beings are doubly active during this time.[87] The inferiority of female child is clearly expressed in the text in stating the double 'uncleanness' period.

Why do we have purification of seven days for a male child and fourteen days for a female child? There are two main opinions: Rabbi Simeon ben Yohai, Hoffmann, and Shadal argue that the seven days for a male child is to have circumcision on the eighth day for which holiness is needed. Rabbi Simeon ben Yohai believes that originally like female child, mother of a male child too was impure for fourteen days, but that was reduced to seven to allow circumcision on the eighth day. For Walter C. Kaiser, 'the circumcision of her son cuts her days of purification in half.'[88] However, the other possibility is the practice among the Hittites, where the impurity for the mother

---

[87] A. W. Streane and A. T. Chapman, *The Book of Leviticus* (Cambridge: University Press, 1914), 67. N. H. Snaith, "Leviticus and Numbers," in *The Century Bible*, ed. H. H. Rowley (London: Thomas Nelson and Sons Ltd, 1967), 90-91.

[88] Kaiser, "The Book of Leviticus," 1084. Besides these, there are many other opinions. One of the opinion laid down are that both the female, mother and newborn daughter are more vulnerable. The mother's loss of blood and even daughter who will lose in future some of her life leaves them weakened and potentially to death. The male also by losing semen experiences the same risk, however, the circumcision on the eighth day protect them from the risk as they enjoy the covenant with God. If so, the woman is vulnerable as she has not received the privilege of being a covenant partner. The male members are the covenant partners with God, and female members are considered as partners with their male counterpart. The woman's rights and status are governed by the male members of the household. Hence, it could be the rationale of the priest and lawmaker. The other possible reason is to separate the Israelites from any connection to the idolatrous fertility rituals practiced by the nations around them (See Alexi E. George, "Leviticus," in *South Asia Bible Commentary*. ed. Brian Wintle (Udaipur: Open Door Publications, 2015), 155.

giving birth to a male child was shorter than that of a female.[89] If the seven days is resulted due to circumcision, it is considered as a holy ritual. The pertinent argument then is, if circumcision makes way for a male child to purity, then what about the female child, for whom no such rite is performed? Does it have to do with Hittite practice? That could be a possibility as seventh day ritual for a new-born was practised among the Hittites.[90] Some argue that the longer period of impurity in case of a girl child is due to ancient belief that women will be subjected by the strong attacks of the demon. Other argument is that the discharges in case of a girl last longer than male. It has also been suggested that the birth of a female child was considered less valuable and therefore, required longer period.[91] The text is not clear. The possibility appears to be the social standing of female, where women are placed much lower than that of men.

The days of impurity for a mother bearing a male child is altogether 40 days (v. 2 –seven days and v.4-thirty three days). The number 40 was one of the chief sacred numbers before the exile (See Exod 24:18).[92] The number 40 is not only prevalent in the scripture, but also in many other cultures such as Greek and Persians. The rules of separation from religious rites are also found in Hittites and in India, though the period of 40 is not practised. However, in Israel a difference can be seen. In Israel, only the mother is considered impure, whereas in Hittite and many other cultures both the child and mother are impure.[93] But if she bears a female child, the impurity period for a mother bearing a female child is double than that of a

---

[89] Jacob Milgrom, "Leviticus 1-16," in *The Anchor Bible*, ed. William Foxwell Albright and David Noel Freedman (New York: Doubleday, 1991), 744, 750. See also Samuel E. Balentine, "Leviticus," in *Interpretation*, ed. Patrick D. Miller (Louisville: John Knox Press, 2002), 100-102.

[90] Milgrom, "Leviticus 1-16," 744.

[91] Frank H. Gorman, "Divine Presence and Community: A Commentary on the Book of Leviticus," in *International Theological* Commentary, ed. Fredrick Carlson Holmgren and George A. F. Knight (Edinburgh: The Handsel Press, 1997), 79; Hartley, "Leviticus," 167.

[92] J. R. Porter, "Leviticus," in *The Cambridge Bible Commentary*, ed. A. R. C. Leaney P. R. Ackroyd, J. W. Packer (London: Cambridge University Press, 1976), 94.

[93] Milgrom, "Leviticus 1-16," 750.

male child (fourteen days and sixty six days). The reason for such prolonged uncleanness as mentioned earlier, is probably due to the attack by the demons.[94] The text gives no explicit answer.

Though the distinction aspect for impurity is stated in the preceding verses, the offerings to be brought for either son or daughter are same. The issue in this verse is asking a woman and not her husband to bring sacrifice after childbirth. The confinement of a woman and thereafter offering possibly points to her as a sinner. The text is silent in this issue. The silence points to a male dominated tradition where woman are subjected to confinement. The text here is not clear, but in the episode of Hannah, she appeared in the sanctuary at Shiloh only when her son Samuel is weaned (I Sam 1:22). When the priest offers both the burnt offering and sin offering and makes atonement on her behalf, then only she will be cleaned from her flow of blood and is eligible to make contact with the sacred objects. The mother bearing male child has to separate herself for 40 days and make an offering to become clean, and in case of bearing female child, she has to dissociate for 80 days and offering, which clearly brings out the picture of confinement and domination.

Why should a birth cause such a prolonged uncleanness which even makes her in confinement? The practice of confinement can be seen in many other cultures. As mentioned earlier, in the Hittite culture, both the child and mother are considered impure. The purification period for the female in the Hittite like biblical culture is longer in comparison to the male.[95]

The rituals laid down by the priest show clearly the status of women in ancient Israel. This practice is found in different cultures

---

[94] Wenham, "The Book of Leviticus," 187. Various reasons are proposed by the scholars. See also C. F. Keil, "The Pentateuch," in *Commentary on the Old Testament*, ed. C. F. Keil and F. Delitzsch (Massachusetts: Hendrickson Publishers, 2001), 571; Mark F. Rooker, "Leviticus," in *The New American Commentary*, ed. E. Ray Clendenen (Nashville: Broadman & Holman Publishers, 2000), 183; Allen P. Ross, *Holiness to the* Lord (Grand Rapids, Michigan: Baker Academic Press, 2002), 267.

[95] Milgrom, "Leviticus 1-16," 763-765. In Indian culture too especially in Manu, all relatives of a new-born child and the house are considered as impure (Manu 5.58). The Hindu women are barred from temples and are confined inside the house during their menstrual period.

throughout the world. It is a universal issue that has evoked criticism positively and negatively throughout the globe. Since holiness is a cultural-historical issue, probably the nations around Israel considered holiness as a supreme duty. Probably Israel (Priestly class) too got influenced by the thinking of her neighboring cultures. This disparaging approach can be supported by chapter 27:1-7, where the redemption price of a female is half of that of man.

The women play crucial role in the procreative activity. They are in a way playing a dominant role in the generative process entrusted by God. Hence, woman must not be intrinsically treated as inferior beings susceptible to danger, rather a key person in continuing the plan and promise of God. The birth of a female child and thereby doubling of the time is not a sign of lesser social standing. All these ritual and practices were perhaps a creation of male dominated society. The role of priests can't be negated, as they were holding an important role in the Israelite society.

Leviticus 15:16-31 - Law on Uncleanness from Bodily Emissions

Translation/Textual Comments

16 And if a man has an emission of semen, he shall bathe his whole body in water and he will be unclean[96] until the evening. 17 And every cloth and every skin that has semen on it will be washed with water and will be unclean until the evening. 18 And a woman[97] with

[96] The projection of semen as unclean marks the differences between Israel and Ancient West Asian legislation. In Ancient West Asian legislation, sexual activity was performed within the sacred precincts among the worshippers as it was believed that such an act would activate the gods into fertilizing the soil with rain (Rooker, "Leviticus," 203).

[97] Samaritan Hebrew Pentateuch reads אִישָׁהּ 'her husband' instead of אִישׁ 'man' (MT reading). In MT, woman is placed as the subject even though her case begins in next verse. If we observe carefully, the law starts with abnormal male discharges followed by normal male discharges. With a break of one verse (v.18), start the normal female discharges instead of abnormal discharges (ab-b1a1). This chiasmus brings out the unity of the text. The centre verse (v.18) instead of beginning with man followed by woman, goes the other way and instead of word כִּי uses the word

whom a man lies and has an emission of semen, both of them shall bathe in water, and they will be unclean until the evening.

19 When a woman has a discharge of blood which is her regular discharge from her body, she will be in her impurity for seven days,[98] and whoever touches her[99] will be unclean until the evening.[100] 20 And everything upon which she lies during her impurity will be unclean; everything upon which she sits will be unclean. 21 And whoever touches her bed shall wash his clothes and bathe with water[101] and will be unclean until the evening. 22 And whoever touches anything[102] upon which she sits[103] shall wash his clothes and bathe in water, and will be unclean until the evening; 23 whether it[104] is the bed or anything upon which she sits, when he touches it he will be unclean until the evening. 24 And if any man[105] lies[106] with

---

אֲשֶׁר (v. 2, 16, 19 and 25). It is purposefully structured by the legislator showing a well-balanced law. Hence, the MT reading is valid.

[98] Seven days is the normal period of the menstrual flow.

[99] It means contact with her body.

[100] The instruction to take bathe is missing (cf. 21, 22). Probably it is a scribal error.

[101] The MT has 'bathe with water' whereas Septuagint adds τὸ σῶμα αὔτου 'his body' i.e bathe his body with water [verse 21 καὶ πᾶς ὃς ἐὰν ἅψηται τῆς κοίτης αὐτῆς πλυνεῖ τὰ ἱμάτια αὐτοῦ καὶ λούσεται τὸ σῶμα αὐτοῦ ὕδατι καὶ ἀκάθαρτος ἔσται ἕως ἑσπέρας].

[102] The Samaritan Hebrew Pentateuch, Targum and Targum Pseudo-Jonathae secundum adds article on כְּלִי.

[103] 'בכָל־כְּלִי אֲשֶׁר־תֵּשֵׁב עָלָיו (anything upon which she sits)' is absent in Targum.

[104] The Samaritan Hebrew Pentateuch reads היא in place of הוא (MT reading). For Hartley the word הוא refers not to a specific antecedent, but to a situation (See Hartley, "Leviticus," 204). See also also for further detail Milgrom, "Leviticus 1-16," 938-939. It refers to any uncontaminated object.

[105] Refer verse 18.

[106] 'If a man *lies* with her…' The word 'שָׁכַב' is in Qal infinite absolute and is placed before יִשְׁכַּב which is in Qal imperfect form. When the infinite absolute is placed before an imperfect form, it intensifies the verbal idea emphasizing the importance of the circumstance (cf. Gen. 2:17- מוֹת תָּמוּת).

her and her impurity is on him, and he becomes unclean[107] seven
days; and every bed on which he lies will be unclean.

25 If a woman has a discharge of blood for many days, not at
the time of her impurity, or if she has a discharge beyond the time
of her impurity, all the days of the discharge she shall continue in
uncleanness; as in the days of her impurity, she will be unclean. 26
Every[108] bed on which she lies all the days of her discharge will be to
her as the bed of her impurity; and everything on which she sits will
be unclean, as in the uncleanness of her impurity. 27 And whoever[109]
touches them[110] will be unclean and he shall wash his clothes, and
bathe in water, and will be unclean until the evening. 28 And when
she is cleansed of her discharge, she shall count off seven days, and
after that she will be clean. 29 And on the eighth day she[111] shall
take two turtledoves or two young pigeons, and bring them to the
priest at the entrance of the tent of meeting. 30 And the priest shall
offer one for a sin offering and the other for a burnt offering; and the
priest will make atonement for her before the Lord for her unclean
discharge.

31 You shall separate[112] the sons of Israel from their uncleanness,
so that they do not die in their uncleanness by defiling my tabernacle
that is in their midst.

---

[107] The Samaritan Hebrew Pentateuch reads יטמא 'he becomes unclean' instead of וְטָמֵא 'and he becomes unclean'. This variant is based on the frequent confusion of *waw* and *yod* at the various stages of the Hebrew scripture (cf. Verse 8a) [refer Hartley, "Leviticus," 204.] This judgement is in contrast with 20:18, where the punishment for both party is cut off. The holiness code is harsh towards both the man and the woman.

[108] A few Hebrew manuscripts Septuagint (textus Graecus originalis), Syriac and Targum Pseudo-Jonathae secundum have waw at the beginning of the verse.

[109] Two manuscripts and Septuagint omits copula (the vav).

[110] Few manuscripts and Septuagint read בה 'her' instead of בם 'them'.

[111] The woman is holding a significant stand in Israel's cult like man where she is having access to make an offering.

[112] The verb וְהִזַּרְתֶּם is in Hiphil form which means ' to cause that a person keeps detached from uncleanness. Probably to be read with Samaritan Hebrew manuscripts and Syriac as והִזְהַרתם 'You will warn'. Septuagint reads καὶ εὐλαβεῖς ποιήσετε 'and you will show discretion/prudence (c.f. Hartley, "Leviticus," 204).

Comments and Explanation

Chapter 15 like chapter 12 deal with genital discharges and the general opinion among the scholars is that both the texts can be joined together.

Chapter 15 deals with male and female discharges. Both sections (2-17 and 19-30) are dependent to each other and are considered as mirror to each other as the language and content are same. In between these two sections verse 18 is placed which deals with marital intercourse. Verse 18 stands as the rhetoric center of the two main sections where ruling on sexual intercourse between a man and a woman is stated. In this chapter, women are not alone placed as unclean because of their discharges, but also men. Men or women with discharges are unclean, contaminating anyone who touches them and anything he or she touches. They require ritual purification for restoration and to lead a normal life. The only difference is the duration. For male, in normal discharge until evening but for female, the time period is 7 days. Though the woman's impurity lasted seven days, no purificatory rite is proposed or demanded.[113] For abnormal case, after healing, both male and female have to wait seven days followed by a purification and burnt offering on the eighth day.

Though the laws are straightforward and are equally placed both for man and woman, it is difficult to understand the logic behind all these rituals, as to have a bodily discharge is a normal condition for human kind. This is what even the creator had intended for human kind. If so, why do the bodily discharges make someone unclean? Is this ritual known only to Israel or prevalent to other cultures? The rituals for discharges are found in almost every culture (Egyptians, Hittite, Babylonian, Arab, Persians, Greeks, and even Hinduism).[114] The entire ancient world is unanimous in this regard.

In this law, once again we can see the priestly dominance where the advantages are for man who imposes harsh social and religious control over women. The form of discrimination was also seen in Gospel writings. It is remarkable to note that Jesus like other Jewish rabbi did not rebuke the woman suffering from bleeding for long

---

[113] Porter, "Leviticus," 121.

[114] Milgrom, "Leviticus 1-16," 932, 957-968.

12 years, when she touched Jesus (Mt 9:20-21; Mk 5:25-33; Lk 8:43-48). The approach of Jesus was contrary to the Levitical laws. In the eyes of Jesus, the standing of women was weightier than the stipulated and rigid regulation.

Leviticus 19:20-22, 29 - Laws for Holy Living

Translation/Textual Comments

20 If a man sleeps[115] with a woman who is a slave, betrothed to another man but not ransomed[116] or given her freedom, an inquiry shall be held.[117] They shall not be put to death,[118] because she was not free; 21 but he shall bring a guilt offering for himself to the Lord, to the door of the tent of meeting, a ram for a guilt offering. 22 And the priest shall make expiation[119] for him with the ram of the guilt offering before the Lord for his sin which he has committed; and the sin which he has committed shall be forgiven him.

29 Do not degrade your daughter by making her a prostitute, so that the land may not turn to prostitution and the land shall be full of depravity.[120]

---

[115] The Hebrew word שִׁכְבַת־זֶרַע means carnal relations.

[116] The MT וְהָפְדֵּה is a hophal infinitive absolute (c.f. 2 Kings 3:23). For Hartley, since the verb הָפְדֵּה stands before a verb נִפְדָּתָה which is in Niphal perfect form, it is more meaningful to repoint it as a niphal infinitive absolute. The Infinitive absolute is used to emphasize the contract. The hophal form communicates both that her owner is duty-bound to let her be redeemed and that her would be is duty-bound to pay the price for redemption (Hartley, 305.). c.f. Milgrom, "Leviticus 17-22", 1667.

[117] The Samaritan Hebrew Pentateuch adds לו 'to him' and Septuagint adds αὐτοῖς 'to them'.

[118] The MT has the verb in Hophal plural form, whereas the Samaritan Hebrew Pentateuch reads a singular form. The following verses support the singular form '*he* shall bring a guilt offering for *himself* (v. 21) and 'the priest shall make atonement for *him* ...... for *his* sin which *he* committed; and the sin which *he* has committed shall be forgiven *him*' (v. 22). Since these two verses point seven times to the ravisher, the proposed translation must be 'he shall not be put to death'.

[119] Wiped clean of impurities.

[120] The Hebrew word זִמָּה 'to plot or conspire' usually refers either to sexual immorality or, as a metaphor to Israel's infidelity in community idolatry [Baruch A.

Comments and Explanation

Verses 20-22 and 29 are placed under miscellaneous duties (vv. 19-29). These laws are about man's relationships with animal, field, garment (v.19), slave woman (vv. 20-22), land (vv. 23-25), body (vv. 26-28) and daughter (v. 29). The laws on slave woman and daughter are placed along with other properties.

Verses 20-22 - The Betrothed Slave Woman

The laws in verses 20-22 is related to the seventh commandment as it has to do with adultery, but since the victimized person is a slave woman and not received freedom, the accused person got escaped from death penalty.

The slave woman in this text is not a freed person. Now, if she had been freed, the law would have been different i.e., death penalty (*they shall not be put to death* cf. Deut 22:23-27). And if she was not betrothed, there would have been no penalty, as the slave was treated as property/chattel. Who is the man who had sexual relation with the slave woman? Is he the owner, member of his household or a person not connected to the owner? The man who had sexual relations with her probably is her owner or member of her owner's household. If not, the penalty would have been paid to her owner, as it has caused a loss to her master.[121] Few questions to be answered: The slave woman is betrothed but not freed, if so, who controls her? Owner or the one to whom she was betrothed! Why the law of adultery is not applicable? Is it because of her position in the society? A closer scrutiny is warranted.

Unlike Deuteronomy where it opts for death (Deut 22:22-25), the law here recommends for an inquiry. The prospective husband must have the same rights as the actual marriage, and

---

Levine, "Leviticus," in *The Jewish Publication Society Torah Commentary*, ed. Nahum M. Sarna (Jerusalem: The Jewish Publication Society, 1989), 122].

[121] Levine, "Leviticus," 131. There are two opinions among the scholars: One opinion argues that the accused man is none other than her owner and the other argument disagrees by stating that if owner, the text would have read 'if a man has sexual relations with a woman *who is his slave*'. Now, if we disagree that the accused man is the owner, the pertinent question will be, why the text does not point compensation to the owner?

having sexual relation with a betrothed girl is adultery and is liable to death penalty.[122] But here the punishment is not death, as she is not redeemed or freed. This clearly shows the power of her ravisher both in the social and economic spheres and a woman wholly at the disposal of her owner.

Verse 29-Daughter and the Land

In this verse, the daughter is equated with the land. Profaning a daughter by making her a prostitute will yield the land to prostitution and depravity. The questions here are: Is it referring to a cultic prostitution or secular one? Who is this daughter? The daughter is an Israelite. Probably an Israelite due to heavy debt was tempted to sell his daughter into prostitution to clear his debt. This form of practice may even tempt the greedy father to sell off his daughter to accumulate wealth, which in turn defiles the land.

The Old Testament has ample references of cultic prostitution (Gen. 38:20-23; Deut 23:17-18; I Kings 14: 23-24; 15:11-12; 22:47; II Kings 23:7; Hos 4:13-14). What made the woman to prostitution? Is it practiced to have fertility rites? The text is not clear. This form of practice was customary among the Canaanites, where a father devoted his daughter.[123] There is a possibility that the Israelite got influenced by the Canaanite cult.

Why did the text narrate 'Do not *degrade* your daughter by making her as a *prostitute*? 'The word 'degrade' and 'prostitute' is a deliberate choice to deprive the right of the woman. This double word is throwing her away from her rights. It brings out the rights and vested interest of her father. Her reputation is completely diminished.

The law in Leviticus takes it in a lighter way unlike the Deuteronomic code, where it is condemned and considered as abhorrent to the Lord (Deut 23:18-19 c.f. Hos 4:14; Amos 2:7).

---

[122] C.f. Wenham, "The Book of Leviticus," 270.

[123] Kaiser, "The Book of Leviticus," 1135; Noth, *Leviticus*, 143. For Porter, cultic prostitution was the object of promoting fertility, and hence the reason for prohibition is primarily religious rather than moral (Porter, "Leviticus," 158).

Lev 25:39-46 - Laws on Slavery

Translation/Textual Comments

39 If your brother becomes poor beside you, and sells himself/sold[124]
to you, you shall not make him serve[125] as slave. 40 As a resident
hireling he shall be with you. He shall serve with you until the year of
the jubilee; 41 Then he shall go out from you,[126] he and his children
with him go back to his own family and to the possession of his
father he shall return. 42 For they are my servants, whom I brought
forth out of the land of Egypt, they shall not be sold as slaves are sold.
43 You shall not rule[127] over him with harshness,[128] but shall fear
your God.[129] 44 As for your male and your female slaves[130] whom
you may have, you may acquire male and female slaves from among
the nations that are around you. 45 You may also buy from among
the strangers who sojourn with you and their families that are with
you, who have been born in your land; and they shall become your
property. 46 You may keep them as a possession for your children
after you, for them to inherit as property. These you may make them
slaves[131] for life, but as for your fellow Israelites, no one shall rule
over the other with harshness.

---

[124] The verb נִמְכַּר is in niphal perfect form. This verb is also read and translated in reflexive (Hithpael) form (cf. v. 47-48).

[125] The MT reads תַעֲבֹד בּוֹ 'you shall make him serve' whereas the Septuagint reads δουλεύσει σοι 'he will serve you'.

[126] Unlike Exodus 21:2 and Deut 15:12, the word חָפְשִׁי 'free' is purposefully omitted as he is treated as hireling and not as a slave.

[127] In Septuagint the word used is κατατενεῖς (hold down right). The word here means 'drive hard'.

[128] This verb means 'ruthlessly'. The meanings in Aramaic, Arabic and Akkadian is mentioned by Milgrom, "Leviticus 23-27," 2227-2228.

[129] MT has מֵאֱלֹהֶיךָ 'your God'. The Septuagint has κύριον τὸν θεόν σου 'the Lord your God' (c.f. Verse 17a).

[130] The Samaritan Hebrew Pentateuch reads as plural, whereas MT read singular (cf. 6a-a).

[131] The words בָּהֶם תַּעֲבֹדוּ 'you may make them slaves' is absent in Septuagint.

Comments and Explanation

The Law on slavery in Holiness Code differs from the parallel codes (Exod 21:2-11 and Deut 15:12-18). In the Covenant Code, the freedom is for the male slave after 7 years and in Deuteronomy code, the freedom is entitled both for male and female slaves after the same duration. The Holiness code is totally different in relation to nature and time duration. If a debtor enters the household of the creditor, his status will be not that of slave but of a resident hireling. They shall serve until the year of jubilee. Then he and his children are to be released. The method of release is identical to buying back one's own land (25:25-28). However, the non-Israelites be treated as property/slaves.

In the Holiness code, there are major differences between an Israelite slave and a non-Israelite slave. The Israelite must not be treated as slave but as a hireling (vv. 39-40) whereas the non-Israelite can be bought and be treated as slave (vv. 44-45). In the year of Jubilee, the Israelite and his family are released as they are freed from the land of Egypt by Lord God (vv. 41-42) whereas for the non-Israelite there is no freedom as they are owner's property (vv. 45-46). The Israelites shall not be ruled with harshness which is mentioned twice (vv. 43, 46), which emphasizes the preference of Israelite over non-Israelite. The treatment for a non-Israelite is not specified, which possibly implies that the owner has every right upon them.

The Holiness Code unlike the Book of Covenant Code and Deuteronomic code promotes for Jubilee instead of 7 year period. For Levine, the law in Leviticus is most severe comparing the parallel codes and allows for almost lifelong indenture.[132] Moreover, the law misses out the redemption or self-redemption clauses. The text even misses out to state the possibility of a relative who can redeem him by paying off his debt. Even there is no indication of the redeemer who is reluctant to redeem him.[133] It is surprising to note that the redemption provision is mentioned to only property (vv. 25-33) and to an Israelite who falls into slavery to an alien (vv. 47-52). The redemption for an Israelite who falls into slavery to an Israelite owner

---

[132] Levine, "Leviticus," 179.

[133] See Milgrom, "Leviticus 23-27," 2216-2217.

is not specified. Is it purposefully missed out? If not, will the Israelite love to fall into slavery to an alien or to an Israelite where there is no redemption clause? The clause in vv. 39-46 is not justified to the cause and welfare of the debtor. It is highly colonial in nature where the powerful/center plays an upper hand over his fellow brethren who are in the margins. Though the debtor is treated not as slave but as hireling, he/she has no freedom until the Jubilee.

The Jubilee release is not applicable to foreign slaves (vv. 44-46). A clear discrimination is seen here. A theological reason underlies for it. God redeemed his people from Egyptian slaves, to become his slaves (vv. 42, 55). It is therefore unfitting, that an Israelite should be resold into slavery, especially to a foreigner.[134]

Here comes the indiscrimination between the native and the Israelite slaves. The Israelites servant must not be treated harshly, and in order to treat harshly, the law permits them to take the slaves from neighboring countries. The native slaves are considered as property (chattel slaves). They are to be passed from generation to generation, as other properties. They will be permanent slaves.

The year of Jubilee was a year of restoration. The people who lost the land received back the land. The land which was in the hand of the rich and powerful has been given back to the original owner. This aspect of restoration can be seen in Persian Imperialism. The Persian Empire instead of deporting the captive people brought the captive people back to their own land. They were given freedom to practice their own religion. The aspect of restoration can be seen both in the year of Jubilee and in the strategy of Persian Imperialism.

Summary

The Holiness Code should not be merely read as a set of rituals and regulations to certify the unclean people as clean, rather to promote a society where people irrespective of class and gender can reach to a stage where their identity is recognized. The society of co-existence leads to wholeness and completeness.

If we go little further, the timing of the Code also matters. The Holiness Code though has elements of pre-monarchic and monarchic

[134] Wenham, "The Book of Leviticus," 322.

times, reached its present state during Persian imperialism. The Persian regime unlike Assyria and Babylon was more open to smaller nations. The Persian Empire adopted strategies different from Assyria and Babylon. Unlike Assyrian and Babylonian strategies of deportation and replacing the land with people of other nations (II Kings 17:6, 24-27), the Persian Empire greatly encouraged the people to return to their homeland. They adopted the strategy of rebuilding and resettling instead of deportation. The Persian regime permitted the people of other nations to worship their god/gods. They even helped in restoring or reconstructing the temple. Freedom was given to exercise their faith and ritual practices.[135] The religion and priesthood in Judah got restored under Persian Empire. The strategy of freedom and restoration adopted by the Persian Empire, on one hand, was to make their boundaries strong and on the other hand, to extract tribute and loyalty from the conquered nations.[136] The intention behind freedom and restoration was to dominate Judah both politically and economically.

The Holiness Code had a strong influence of Persian imperialism, as it gave the people of Judah a new sense of identity. The office of priesthood regained their former strength and glory. The high priest had upper hand over the community. With the support of priest, the rich people enjoyed the privileges of the Persian Empire. This created a gap between the powerful/center and the powerless/margin. It had its effect on the weaker sections of the society specially the women and the slave.

In our observation, the Holiness Code falls after the Covenant and Deuteronomic code. Though it falls closely with the Covenant Code, however, in few cases it has resemblances with the Deuteronomic code. While the Holiness code emphasizes on holiness and the penalty laid down is either death or cut off from the community, the yardstick adopted for women specially the female slaves differs from the male. For instance, a superficial reading shows

---

[135] Martin Noth, *The History of Israel* (London: Adam and Charles Black, 1960), 302.

[136] Jon L Berquist, *Judaism in Persian's Shadow: A Social and Historical Approach* (Eugene, Origen: Wipf and Stock Publishers, 1995), 25-26.

that the laws in relation to female slave are almost similar to the Covenant Code where she is considered as the property of the owner (Lev 20:20-22 c.f. Exod 21:7-11). Nevertheless, in some cases, the holiness code stands much better than the Covenant Code, for instance the freedom of female slave. In the Covenant Code, the freedom for female slave is not specified. In the deuteronomic Code, the freedom is both for the male and female slave. In Holiness Code, the freedom is both for Hebrew male and female slave with few differences. Nonetheless, the time period in Holiness Code differs from the other two codes and the treatment between Hebrew and non-Hebrew slaves are clearly specified in the Holiness Code, which is missing in the other two Codes. A closer reading shows that the Holiness code appears to be ambivalent in nature.

In short, the Holiness Code must be read against the period in which it was emerged. It came during the time of restoration. Though, it was a period of blessings for the nation Israel, but it was not so for the people in margin, as they were treated differently by the people of the center. The wholeness and completeness comes only when all enjoy freedom and becomes the participants in shaping and promoting the society.

The Deuteronomic Code and the Community

Within the legal Codes of the Pentateuch, unlike that of men, the position of margins particularly women is varied, as the Deuteronomic Code differs from the Covenant Code. In the Covenant Code, male and female are subjected to different sets of rules. It enforces the degradation of women and inscribes male power. The legal terminology used when dealing with women and their sexuality is concerned far more with property than with gender. The laws in the Deuteronomy Code however, had a progressive and positive concern for the legal status of women, which is not found in the Covenant Code. The laws in the Holiness Code are more or less ambivalent in nature.

Some of the areas need to be addressed are: How far are the alien cultures and practices enmeshed in the Israelite legal system? Did the existing law codes undergo a change or development in the course of her history? Did the changes occur due to the repeated foreign invasions in the course of her history? Is the language of female subordination limited to patriarchy only or is it impacted by colonialism also?

A good number of scholars have studied extensively the Israelite law system. These works shed light on the subordination of women in religious and other spheres of life. For example, Phyllis Bird[137] sees the subordination of women as the result of patrilineal and patriarchy. She therefore advocates a reconstruction of traditional historiography devoid of the above. Anderson[138] argues by raising two important questions: Did the laws serve a legal purpose? Can Ancient Israelite society be reconstructed from the biblical laws? She answers these questions by employing Gender and Postmodern Feminist Legal theory. G. I. Emmerson[139] has emphasized the subordination of women in the Old Testament arguing that the women played a crucial role in the liberation and progression of Israel, but they were not given due credit. Victor Matthews'[140] analyses the law and points out the protective and positive attitude towards women in the Deuteronomic law code. Habel[141] advocates a sociological approach. His argument is to read the text by identifying with the oppressed group. Chirchigno's[142] approach is more of a comparative analysis. The arguments of all these scholars in general are based on patrilineal

---

[137] Phyllis Bird, "The Place of Women in the Israelite Cultus," in *Ancient Israelite Religion*, Miller Patrick (ed.), Philadelphia: Fortress Press, 1987, 397-419.

[138] Cheryl B. Anderson. Women, Ideology and Violence: Critical Theory and the Construction of the Gender in the Book of the Covenant and the Deuteronomic Law. London: T& T Clark, 2004.

[139] G. I. Emmerson, "Women in Ancient Israel." In The World of Ancient Israel: Sociological, Anthropological and Political Perspectives, R. E. Clement (ed.), Cambridge: Cambridge University Press, 1989, 371-394.

[140] Victor H. Matthews, Bernard M. Levinson, and Tikva Frymer-Kensky. *Gender and Law in the Hebrew Bible and the Ancient Near East.* Sheffield: Sheffield Academic Press, 1998.

[141] N. C. Habel. "The Future of Social Justice Researching the Hebrew Scriptures: Questions of Authority and Relevance." In *Old Testament Interpretation: Past, Present and Future,* London: T & T Clark, 1995, 277-291.

[142] Gregory C. Chirichigno. *Debt-Slavery in Israel and the Ancient Near East,* Journal for the Study of the Old Testament Supplement Series 141. Sheffield: Sheffield Academic Press, 1993.

and patriarchal ideology. They bring out the discrepancy in the law codes and express their reservation against domination both in class and gender. Many other scholars have also contributed immensely to the understanding of the Israelite law system such as Bernard Levinson (Levinson argues for revision and interpolation).The issues raised by all these scholars and their contributions are immensely helpful to locate the reasons behind the degradation of the weaker sections in the society which includes slaves and women.

The issue before us is to find out whether female subordination was exclusively due to patriarchal ideology or it has a colonial dimension also. This section intends to find out whether there is any power play (Colonial interest) within and outside of Israel in shaping/formation of the Israelite legal system, which affected the weaker sections of the society especially women. This section will also attempt to address the position of women in India.

To address this issue, the writer will take the help and insight of subaltern readings along with other readings which support the people of the margins for their rights to life, equality and self-determination. The Subaltern reading advocates who write history from below feel that the histories of the rural peasantry, working class, and women were documented first by the colonial powers and then rewritten by the elite social groups to meet their terms and interest. The biblical law codes derived strong influence from the neighboring powerful nations like Assyria, Babylon and Persia. This view can be substantiated through the differences in the law codes.

The following section will be a comparative study of selected laws focusing primarily on people of *marginalia.*

Selected Texts from Deuteronomic Code

The law played a key role in the life of Israel. It provided the framework for legal decisions. Though it is not complete, it enabled the executors to govern the daily life of Israel.

Historical Background

It is generally agreed that the Deuteronomic Code (12-26), though widely regarded as the 'original' Deuteronomy and the oldest part of the book of Deuteronomy, is a product of Josiah's reform (this view is endorsed by Martin Noth and others). If we agree this view, the political changes occurred during that era has much significance. The law and the reformation had a strong bearing on the weakening and collapse of the Assyrian control over Judah. For a century, Assyria had control over Judah (736/733 BCE- 630/622 BCE). The Assyrian dominance upon Judah can be seen from the Syro-Ephramite war (736-733 BCE) to Josiah's reform (622 BCE). By the time Josiah came to the throne, the power of Assyria had declined, which probably was a major reason for reformation in Judah (cf. II Kings 22-23). This development also paved the way for Judah to control her sister kingdom Israel. The destruction of the sanctuary at Bethel and the suppression of its priesthood (II Kings 23:15-20) is a clear reference. The rapid decay of the Assyrian world empire must have encouraged Josiah to throw off his vassalage, abandon the agreement made between him and the Assyrian king. Thus, Josiah took full advantage of the weakness of the Assyrian empire and brought oneness in Israel by attaining a separate identity and freedom from external political, social and religious interference. This aspect of oneness can be seen in the book of Deuteronomy. In the light of this political development we can understand better the laws of Deuteronomy and rights of margins. The laws of Deuteronomy unlike other law codes are highly moralistic and humanitarian. The laws are very deeply concerned with the idea of Israel as the nation chosen and redeemed expecting the same attitude towards fellow human beings. The laws unlike the other parallel codes give more importance to the overall social and cultural development of Israel.[143]

Deuteronomy12-26 is the detailed law of the covenant. It deals with the religious life (unity and purity of Israel's worship, sporadic obligations and institutions), political life (the responsibility of the officials of theocratic state towards their nation and vice versa), and

---

[143] The Law deals with the fundamental aspects of family life such as release of both male and female slaves at the end of every seven years (Deut 15:12-18), prohibition against selling a wife, who had been chosen from among captives (Deut 21:14), protection of women in marriage (Deut 22:19). C.f. R. E. Clements, "Deuteronomy," in *Old Testament Guides*, ed. R. N. Whybray (Sheffield: JSOT Press, 1989), 85-93.

social life (respect of individuals particularly in the context of family relationships, humanitarian behavior, first fruits and tithe etc.). Based on the correspondence between some of the laws, for instance Decalogue and slavery, it is proposed and argued by some scholars that Deuteronomic Code is a modification of Exodus Code while others argue that the Deuteronomic Code harmonizes the legislation of Covenant Code and Holiness Code. The writer's interest is not to have a detailed study on these issues, rather to read the text in a subaltern perspective, as it deals with a revolution of freedom to all members of the society irrespective of their class and gender.

Deuteronomy 15:12-18-The Liberation of the Hebrew Slaves

Translation/Textual Comments

12 If your brother[144] Hebrew man or a Hebrew woman is sold to you,[145] he shall serve you six years and in the seventh year you shall let him go free[146] from you.13 And when you send him free from you, you shall not send him out empty-handed;[147] 14 You shall provide him liberally[148] out of your flock, out of your threshing floor,[149] and out of your wine press; You shall give to him as[150]

---

[144] The slave (man or a woman) is considered as a member of the community (Israelite).

[145] Few Versions like NEB prefer 'sells himself or herself to you' (hithpael) instead of 'sold to you' (Niphal). Grammatically both translations are possible. It is interesting to note that the law completely avoids the term 'owner', which clearly shows the brotherly act of responsibility and generosity.

[146] It is a technical term for a special social status, i.e., 'freedman'.

[147] Cf. Gen. 31:42; Exod 3:21.

[148] Lit., put upon the neck. The purpose behind this generosity is to break the cycle of servitude.

[149] Few Hebrew manuscripts and Targum codex manuscripts read without *waw* conjunction.

[150] The Samaritan Hebrew Pentateuch and few other versions read כַּאֲשֶׁר (cf.16:10). MT lost a כ (k) possibly by haplography, as the preceding word ends with a כ.

Yahweh your God[151] has blessed you.15 You shall remember that you were a slave in the land of Egypt, and the Lord your God[152] redeemed you; therefore I command you this word today.[153]16 But if he says to you, "I will not go out from you" because he loves you and your household, since he is well off with you, 17 then you shall take an awl, and thrust it through his ear[154] into the door, and he shall be your slave forever. You shall do the thus (same) likewise to your female slave. 18 It[155] shall not seem hardship to you (your eye)[156] when you send them out from you free, because for six years he has served you worth the wages[157] of hired servant;[158] and the Lord your God will bless you in all that you do.

---

[151] A reading of Hebrew manuscripts from Qumran (I Q Deut) read אדני (Lord) instead of יהוה (Yahweh).

[152] Septuagint adds an adverb ἐκεῖθεν 'from there' [ἐλυτρώσατό σε κύριος ὁ θεός σου ἐκεῖθεν 'Lord your God redeemed from there']

[153] MT adds 'today' but this word is absent in LXX. The IQ Deut, Targum Pseudo Jonathan and Septuagint supplement the word 'to do' after 'commanding you'.

[154] Thrusting the awl through the servant's ear has a symbolic significance such as obligation to obey, attached to the owner's house [Refer Duane L. Christensen, "Deuteronomy 1:1-21:9," in *Word Biblical Commentary*, ed. John D. W. Watts (Nashville: Thomas Nelson Publishers, 2001), 320-321.]

[155] Few manuscripts Samaritan Hebrew Pentateuch, Septuagint, Latin and Syriac add *waw* conjunction at the beginning of the negative particle לֹא.

[156] Septuagint reads preposition with genitive ἐναντίον σου 'before you'. It has been proposed as 'in your eyes'.

[157] It can be translated as 'twice', 'double' or equivalent. The Septuagint translates this verse as "ὅτι ἐφέτιον μισθὸν τοῦ μισθωτοῦ ἐδούλευσέν σοι ἓξ ἔτη'(because he has served you six years for the *annual* wage of a hired man laborer). For more reading on this difficult text refer Christensen, 321; James M. Lindenberger, "How Much for a Hebrew Slave? The Meaning of Misneh in Deut 15:18- Critical Notes," *JBL* 110, no. 3 (1991): 479-498.

[158] AV and KJV reads '...his service has been worth *twice* as much as that of a hired servant'. RSV reads it as 'half'. NRSV reads it as '...worth the wages of hired laborers'. For von Rad and Thompson, the word *misneh* is probably a technical term meaning 'equivalent to' [See Gerhard von Rad, *Deuteronomy* (London: SCM Press Ltd, 1966), 108; J. A. Thompson, *Deuteronomy:An Introduction and Commentary*, ed. D. J. Wiseman, The Tyndale Old Testament Commentaries (England: Inter-Varsity Press, 1974), 191]. For Philips, the Hebrew is uncertain. If twice, then the

Comments and Explanation

The slave law 15:12-18 is casuistic in style[159] and is made up of two sections (vv.12-15a and vv.16-18). Verse 15b stands as the center of the literary unit emphasizing the reason to redeem the indentured servant. Each of these sections has a law in casuistic form followed by an exhortation (v. 15 and v.18).[160]

The law in Deuteronomy advocates the release of all Israel's slaves after a period of six years. Moreover, at the time of release, the owner must not send him with empty hand, rather must provide him a generous provision. The people should show empathy to those who have been forced into servitude due to difficult circumstances.[161] However, in spite of this provision, the slaves are free to remain with their masters for life. It totally contradicts the law of release in the Book of the Covenant (Exod 21:2-11).

This law provides remission to those who have lost their freedom because of debt and poverty. It refers to debt slaves and not foreign slaves. The Hebrew man or woman after serving as a slave for six years must be freed on the seventh year and the owners are expected to provide them liberally so that they may start a new and independent life. As saving and sacrificial love of the Lord God was bestowed upon the people of Israel in Egypt, when they were weak and enslaved, hence they are expected to do so with their fellow brethren.

---

normal three year contract of hire is being contrasted with six year of slavery. The 19th century BCE Babylonian code of Lipit-Ishtar provides the release of a debtor once he had given services equivalent to twice the amount of his debt. The Code of Hammurabi granted release after three years [see Philips, 106-107. Peter C. Craige, *The Book of Deuteronomy* (Grand Rapids, Michigan: William B. Eerdmans Publishing Company, 1976), 238-239].

[159] Unlike the impersonal style, which is a typical form in Casuistic style, here it is in second person singular form.

[160] A. D. H. Mayes, "Deuteronomy," in *New Century Bible Commentary*, ed. Ronald E. Clements (Grand Rapids, Michigan: Wm. B. Eerdmans Publishing Company, 1979), 252.

[161] Christensen, 318. Also refer Victor H Matthews, *Manners and Customs in the Bible* (Massachusetts: Hendrickson Publishers, 1991), 136-138.

Unlike the Covenant Code, the uniqueness of Deuteronomic Code is not just in its change of words 'Hebrew', rather the word 'brother' (verse 12) marks a radical and significant difference from the parallel law codes especially the Covenant Code. Women are also given equal privilege with men in the release (v.12 and 17). These additions mark a significant step from the Covenant Code. The Deuteronomic Code supersedes the Covenant code by granting equal treatment to female.[162] The position of equality clearly shows that the Deuteronomic Law springs from a more advanced stage of society where the power of a father over his daughter was no longer supreme.[163] The one whom you are obliged to free is your fellow brother or sister, which pictures a strong humanitarian concept, where there is no room for 'power over others'. This humanitarian approach is missing in Exodus 21:2-11. In Exodus, the female slave is given a lower status and is in a different footing. For Thompson, a concubine is probably a slave. What is implicit in the Covenant Code becomes explicit in Deuteronomic Code.[164]

The saying, *If a member of your community is sold to you* is in the context of vv. 1-11. The reason for the sale would be due to the default in the repayment of debt. The way to substitute the debt is by servitude. He or she shall serve you six years. These are not the six years of the sabbatical cycle, rather six years following the sale. In the seventh year, they are declared as free.

You shall let him go free- This command is in line with the phrase 'Let my people go' (Exod. 5:1). This expression is a humanistic approach. In Exodus the command stated is 'he shall

---

[162] Jeffrey H. Tigay, "Deuteronomy," in *The Jewish Publication Society Torah Commentary*, ed. Nahum M. Sarna (Jerusalem: The Jewish Publication Society, 1996), 148.

[163] S. R. Driver, "Deuteronomy: A Critical and Exegetical Commentary," in *The International Critical Commentary*, ed. A. Plummer and C. A. Briggs S. R. Driver (Edinburgh: T&T Clark, 1996), 182-183.

[164] Thompson, 189. Also see S. R. Driver, *A Critical and Exegetical Commentary on Deuteronomy* (Edinburgh: T&T Clark, 1902), 182; Meredith G. Kline, *Treaty of the Great King* (Grand Rapids, Michigan: William B. Eerdmans Publishing Company, 1963), 90. For S.R. Driver, the law of Deuteronomy comes from a more advanced society than the law of Exodus.

go out free' (v. 2), whereas here the owner is indebted to release his slave (cf. v. 18).[165] In verses 13-14, the owner is asked to garland the slave, i.e., a necklace of flocks, grain and wine in abundance.[166] The understanding here is to bestow generously.

The Deuteronomic Code goes beyond the provision of Exodus 21:2-11.[167] The obligation aspect is missing in the Covenant Code. Here the owner's responsibility towards the slave is highlighted. The slave would not begin his state of new freedom in destitution, a state of indigent insecurity, rather must enjoy himself or herself as a full and independent member of the society. The strong humanitarian spirit and concern for the weak and the oppressed can be seen clearly. A remarkable advance of social thinking is shown in this text. The principle of love, for God and for fellow human, is vital to the covenant community,[168] and it is strongly demonstrated in this text, but Exodus 21:2-11 makes no provision for the released slaves.

Therefore I command you this word today (V.15) - The word 'today' is unique in the command of freeing the indentured servants. It stands exactly at the center of the literary unit (between two sub units: vv. 12-15a and 16-18).[169] Here the call to remember was not merely a means to evoke sympathy or compassion for the slave, which would lead to generosity, rather to realize their past, when they were slaves under Egypt (Deut. 5:15, 16:12, 24:18, 22). The freedom from the bondage in Egypt was not their merit, rather the love of God towards them. The love of God is shown both by delivering them

---

[165] Moshe Weinfeld, *Deuteronomy and the Deuteronomic School* (Oxford: Clarendon Press, 1972), 282-283.

[166] Wright, 192-193.

[167] For Driver, the regulation of slave respecting the wife and family of a slave (21:3-4) is disregarded in Deuteronomy and is replaced by the provision aspect (See Driver, *A Critical and Exegetical Commentary on Deuteronomy*, 183). For Christenson, in the Exodus narrative, the people received gifts of silver and gold objects from their former masters in Egypt (Refer Christensen, 318).

[168] Craige, 238; Thompson, 190. For Philips, the deuteronomic code actively encourages the slave to claim freedom, and the master has no longer any control over the slave's private life (See Philips, 106). For Wright, the command of generosity is a sign of honor (Wright, 192).

[169] Christensen, 319.

from the hands of Egypt and also by providing ample provisions (cf. Exod. 3:21-22 [you will not go empty-handed], 11:2, 12:25-27).[170] In return, they should do no less to the manumitted slaves in the seventh year. A powerful motivating force is thus indicated. As per our study, comparing this passage with other codes, the proper love and concern of God towards the poor are expressed here. In Exodus, the taste of injustice is seen, especially towards the female slave. Here, the liberation of the male and the female slave is an act of love, whereas in Exodus, it is an act of cruelty. Total justice is seen when a person set free has some hope of success ahead. And if it is not achieved, it is nothing other than leading them to further slavery.

The law intends that freedom be given to all. But, if a slave, in spite of receiving freedom, decides to stay with the owner, he shall be categorized as *perpetual slave* (v.17). The regulation and exhortation contained in vv.12-17 are applied equally to male and female slaves (v. 17b), which are missing totally in Exodus 21. In the Exodus passage, the slaves are brought to God (household gods before whom the ceremony was performed), but Deuteronomy does not mention it. The reason for it is that, gods had been rendered illegal objects under Josiah's reform (II Kings 23:24).[171] The pierced ears indicate to the general public the slave's legal position. It also symbolizes his/her obligation to hear the owner's order. It also served as a slave mark.

Had the slaves been of free service for six years, there would have been every possibility of selfishness and greed on the side of owner. So, here the law clearly indicates that, the six years of service is worth the wages of hired laborers. The slaves had worked for no pay, and the wages that would have been paid to an employee for the same labor were to be considered as full repayment for the debt that had caused the slavery in the first instance.[172] The law here again cautions the owner of the slaves, which had served under them due

---

[170] Refer Eugene H. Merrill, "Deuteronomy," in *The New American Commentary*, ed. E.Ray Clendenen (USA: Broadman & Holman Publishers, 1994), 245-246.

[171] The Deuteronomic legislator avoids the word 'God' rather prefers the word 'door' to highlight the 'single sanctuary' practice and consider the household gods as illegal objects under Josiah's reform. Also see Cairns, 150; Philips, 107.

[172] Craige, 239.

to the debt. So, one should not consider it as hardship, rather free them with total willingness. The result will be blessing from God. This concept is totally absent in the Exodus passage.

Hence, the law of slavery in Deuteronomy is sound both theologically and economically. The economic feasibility to have a new and fresh beginning of life, i.e., a historical and economic redemption (Exod. 12:33-36) is given much emphasis. It recognizes and respects the private life of the slave. The law regards him as a brother, who sells himself/herself his/her service, and not his/her person. Unlike Exodus, there is no mention of the hidden agenda of the owner to increase his slaveholdings by giving the slave a wife and at the end of six years keeping back the wife and children. The slave now has a voice in the community, and as a citizen he enjoys the same rights as his master. He has not only the rights of freedom but also can stay with his family (In the Covenant Code, the slave has to decide whether he needs freedom or family and in Holiness code, children can go with him, but the freedom of wife is not mentioned). The Deuteronomic Code does not view male and female slave as chattel under owner's control, rather as 'brother'/fellow Israelite. Justice and compassion to the weak and powerless members of the community are well addressed in this law.

Deuteronomy 16:11-14 -Worship and Fellowship Meal for All Members of the Society

Translation/Textual Comments

11 And rejoice before the Lord your God, you and your son and your daughter, and your manservant[173] and your maidservant, and the Levite who is within your towns, and the sojourner, and the fatherless and the widow who are among you at the place that the Lord your God will choose to dwell (as a dwelling) for his name. 12
You shall remember that you were a slave in Egypt;[174] and you shall

[173] The Samaritan Hebrew Pentateuch, Septuagint (ὁ παῖς σου) and Vulgate miss out the *vav* conjunction.

[174] Some Hebrew manuscripts like Samaritan Hebrew Pentateuch (מִצְרַיִם בְּאֶרֶץ), Septuagint (ἐν γῇ Αἰγύπτῳ) read 'in the land of Egypt' cf. 5:15. In MT here and in 24:18 בְּמִצְרַיִם (in Egypt) is used.

be careful to observe these decrees. 13 You shall keep the feast of booths (tabernacles) seven days, when you have gathered from your threshing floor and from your wine press; 14 you shall rejoice in your feast, you and your son and your daughter, and your manservant and your maidservant, the Levite, and the sojourner, and the fatherless and the widow who is within your towns.

Comments and Explanation

Deuteronomy 16:1-17 deals with the three feasts of Israel. Within the series of festival, vv1-8 (the feast of Passover) is much discussed as verse 3 contradicts with verse 8. It is generally argued among the scholars that the two feasts, Passover and Unleavened bread have been combined.[175] This chapter consists of the Passover with Unleavened bread (vv.1-8), the feast of Weeks (9-12), the feasts of Booths (13-15) followed by a summary (16-17).The expectation of Yahweh in all these feasts to the people of Israel is to remember the faithfulness of God in their lives, and to observe the feasts from generation to generation by involving 'all members of the society' (vv. 11, 14). This passage is a Deuteronomic version as it gives more importance to worship (the word 'rejoice' is unique in Deuteronomy). The three feasts with the exception of Passover have an agricultural setting and belong to the period of settlement.[176]

The heart of the festival is not merely to remember the salvific act of God and His blessing, but to have a fellowship meal involving 'all members of the community' regardless of their socio-economic status. The law here motivates the owner to extend the celebration to servants and other members connected to his family, i.e., the center and margins having fellowship together with the Creator and Covenant God.

---

[175] Mayes, 254-256. For Christopher Wright, Deuteronomist has woven together Israel's two great feasts with a purpose. It looks back their past and points to the future. The Passover is primarily the celebration of the exodus and the feast of unleavened bread though rooted in Exodus could only be celebrated in the context of land (Wright, 198.). The Deuteronomist makes the three feasts as two with the word 'rejoice' in both of these sections (v. 11 and v. 14).

[176] H. Cunliffe-Jones, "Deuteronomy," in *Torch Bible Commentaries*, ed. Alan Richardson John Marsh, R. Gregor Smith (London: SCM Press Ltd, 1951), 101.

Deuteronomy 16:9-17 deals about the feast of weeks and the feast of booths. Unlike the parallel passages in Exodus (23:14ff. and 34:18ff) and Leviticus (23:15-22, 33-44), Deuteronomic passage has a difference. Neither of the two feasts in Deuteronomy is connected with salvation history (cf. Exod. 23:15; 34: 18; Lev. 23:42-43). In the Book of Leviticus, the dwelling in booths is projected to remind the people of Israel of their wandering in the desert. In the Book of the Covenant the feast of weeks is called as the feast of harvest (23:16).[177] In the Deuteronomic Code, the striking significance is not merely her history, rather the involvement of each member of the society ('Rejoice ...you and your sons and your daughters, your male and female slaves, the Levites, the strangers, the orphans and widows-vv. 11 and 14). In the parallel passages only the male members were given the privilege as they were considered as the members of the covenant community. For the Deuteronomist, the dependent members are given the privilege, as an Israelite too was once in a similar dependent social position (cf. 15:15).[178] Verse 12 is the reason for such stipulation 'Remember that you were a slave in Egypt'. For Deuteronomy, the reason for celebration is not merely to know how they came out of Egypt, i.e., exodus experience, rather how their lives were when they lived in Egypt, i.e., their servitude (Exod. 23:14; Lev. 23:43; Deut 16:12).[179] Since in Egypt all faced the same experience and got deliverance, hence participation in the feast was not limited to male members of the society, rather to all.[180] Each member of the community had access and rights to enjoy the feast. For the Deuteronomist, the festivals were a time of rejoicing for all members of the community. He creates empathy for the

[177] Rad, *Deuteronomy*, 110-113.

[178] Merrill, 254; Philips, 113-114.

[179] For Mayes, the reference to Egypt in the context of this festival is of deuteronomic origin...(Mayes, 260).

[180] In our observation, along with God, there were human agents for the deliverance of Israel. The human agents were not merely the male members of the society, rather people irrespective of sex. Hence, the rights of rejoicing are for all. Surprisingly, the other parallel codes center around the male members of the society. Possibly, the Deuteronomist had that in mind while giving away this particular legislation.

weak and marginalized and creates a sense of feelings among them that they too are given rest to celebrate the redemptive act of God. Hence, the celebration unlike in other codes, gives a new meaning to the community emphasizing the significance of each member irrespective of their social standing. This change is vital as it brings social bonding and renewal, and a deep conviction that they are part of the community of God.

General Observations on Biblical Law Codes

Some of the main observations addressed and needed further researches are:

1. Cultures of Ancient West Asia: A Fusion!

How far the alien cultures and practices got enmeshed Israel?

The Ancient West Asia culture especially of Assyria, Babylon and Israel was a blend of two distinct cultures: The Sumerian culture and Semitic culture. The Sumerian culture was basically matriarchal in nature, where the position of women to some extent was favorable. The dignity of woman was well recognized. They enjoyed the privileges of men, though not of same scale. Semitic culture was patriarchal in nature, where the status of women was of disadvantage, where the father, brother, husband (the male members) of the household played a key role.

Semitic culture in course of time had engrafted some of the elements of the Sumerian culture. Sumerians in turn were subjected to a stronger Semitic influence, ethnically and linguistically. These opposing matriarchal and patriarchal cultures got hybridized resulting in a new culture where discrimination against women continued. In Israelite law, there are references where women were treated well particularly in the Deuteronomic Code; however, the major portions of the laws are unfavorable to women. These differences took place probably due to the fusion of these two cultures.

2. Discrepancies in the Biblical Law Codes

Why do discrepancies in the Biblical Law Codes exist?

Each of the biblical law codes (BC, HC, and DC) is a multifaceted text. The differences in laws especially with regard to weaker groups ask for careful investigation. The acceptance and support of slavery system and the view of women as property ought to be seriously relooked and investigated.

A. Laws on Slavery

All the three biblical codes like AWA codes support the institution of slavery. The harshest among them is the Covenant Code. The Holiness code is much closer and is parallel to the Deuteronomic Code. The pertinent question is: why is the institution of slavery promoted?

1. In the Covenant Code, the slave law starts with 'when you buy a Hebrew slave…' It projects from the view point of a buyer/owner. The Deuteronomic and Holiness code unlike the Covenant Code emphasize the distressed side of the enslaved person ['If your fellow Hebrew, man or woman is sold to you/sell himself to you…(Deut. 15:12)', 'If your fellow brother is reduced to poverty and sells himself to you, you must not use him to work for you as a slave… (Lev 25:39-40)'].
2. In the Deuteronomic Code, freedom for both the male and female slave is on an humanitarian ground and has strong moral and ethical aspects. The owner is expected to provide them liberally to ensure that they may not enter into slavery. Moreover, the law clearly reminds the Israelite community about their past and cites the reason for the freedom of the slaves (Deut 15:15). The Covenant Code gives no room for liberty. Though the male slave can go free in the seventh year, there is no guarantee that he could live an independent life, as he is sent empty handed.
3. The Holiness Code, on the other hand, ensures freedom in a different way (year of Jubilee) which is closer to the Deuteronomic code. The understanding of "Your brother/fellow countryman" is not just for a kinsman but also any fellow Israelite\Hebrew appears to be taken from

> Deuteronomy. The Holiness Code like the Deuteronomic Code instructs the owner to treat the impoverished individual with an open heart (Lev 25:43). They are to be treated not as slave, rather as a hired man. However, it clearly differentiates the Hebrew slaves from the non-Hebrew slaves.

B. Women and Law: Patriarchal and Colonial Ideology

The majority of the laws both the casuistic and apodictic laws address the community through its male members. The law codes in general treat women as property and she is always subjected to the authority of male members of the society. The Covenant Code is much harsher towards women, where they have no right of freedom and are controlled by their male counterparts. The Deuteronomic Code and the Holiness Code to a great extent provide freedom to women. The Covenant Code appears to be in line with the Ancient West Asian Codes (Middle Assyrian Laws, Code of Hammurabi and Eshnunna laws).

The whole of Ancient West Asian laws are patriarchal and colonial in color. Women were constantly addressed and treated as property similar to slaves. The rights and dignity of women were at a low level both in social and religious order. They were directly controlled by the male members of the society. Their sexuality belonged exclusively to her husbands. If she failed to bear a child, he could marry another. The wife in order to safeguard her life was forced to handover a maid to her husband. The law is silent, if the problem of not bearing child lies with the husband. Women were treated as chattel to be bought and sold. The identity of women was limited to that of a daughter to a father, a wife to a husband, a maid to a mistress. In short, women were ignored, despised and subverted.

The Ancient West Asian laws including the Book of the Covenant Code are marked between the powerful and the powerless. In order to amass wealth and maintain superiority over other nations, women were targeted. Land was more important and an integral part in the life of agricultural society. In order to increase labor force, women became tools. In case of war, women taken as captives and were carried by enemies mainly for sexual reasons and to procreate descendants for the triumphant nations. The unprecedented political and economic importance of the colonial power affected the very fabric of the Israelite society, which can be seen in the legal code. The legal code which was supposed to bring justice and welfare to all became a tool of injustice. Israel perhaps in order to compete with other nations mimicked the social departmentalization of her neighboring nation/s.

Hence, the Book of the Covenant Code in particular must be deconstructed and dismantled, which was adapted the political, cultural and religious practice of the neighboring nations, in order to build and construct a new voice to uplift women and the marginalized from the clutches of powerful ideologies of patriarchy and colonialism.

3. Powerful and Powerless: The Power Play behind the Law

Is there any power play behind the promulgation of the laws?

It is generally accepted that the laws of Ancient West Asia had not reached in its present shape initially, rather there was a growth and development based on the changing situation and demands. In all other laws except Israel, the king played the key role behind the promulgation of the laws. In order to make the laws valid, at the very outset they address god/gods with an understanding that the law is binding and applicable to all (for instance, Code of Hammurabi). However, in Israel unlike Ancient West Asian nations, it was not only the king who played the key role behind the community formation and building process, rather the office of the prophet and the Priest too played the key roles. There were frictions between these offices. Throughout the Old Testament prophetical books, we can notice how the prophets attacked the office of kings (for instance, Samuel's rebuke to King Saul), and how they even attacked the priest (Malachi 1:6-2:9; Zephaniah 3:4; Micah 6:6-8). The role of the offices of prophet and priest behind the daily life of Israel which includes the legal tradition cannot be negated, as it brings the people under their control. In a tussle between the powerful, the real victims were those who had no voice to raise and fight for their rights. Women and their rights were thus totally ignored.

Summing up, the Covenant Code probably came to its final shape in the eighth century BCE, a time when Assyrian empire was weak (783-745 BCE)[181] and Israel as a nation was emerging equally competent with the other neighboring nations. The nation of Israel in order to compete with other nations probably modified the legislation which created an immense gulf between the powerful and powerless, which in turn affected the weaker sections especially women. The Deuteronomic Code reached its present form in the seventh century BCE, when the Assyrian Empire was declining. The kings of Judah particularly Manasseh and Josiah took this opportunity to reform the entire system including the legislation. It narrowed down the gap between the rich and the poor. The weaker section particularly women benefited as they too received their rights. The Holiness Code came to its present form during Persian Imperialism (sixth century BCE). The Persian Empire unlike Assyria and Babylon granted the captive people the right to worship and the people of Judah regained their former strength. The Persian strategy was to extend their boundaries and to have leaders of the captive group, which would further strengthen their empire. The governor and high priest of Judah were given power over the Judean community. This privilege created a gulf between the religious leaders and the common people. Holiness and strict regulations were imposed on the people. It affected the common people, especially women. Hence, the Holiness Code is ambivalent in nature.

The writer argues that the Covenant Code appears to have originated or codified during the Assyrian rule (8th century BCE), the Deuteronomic Code toward the end of the Assyrian colonialism and the rise of Babylonian colonial advent (7th century BCE) and the Holiness Code during the Persian colonial period (6th century BCE). So, all Israel's law system, at least their codifications took place under the colonial experiences of the people of God. These experiences vary in their intensity: the Assyrian conquest and its colonial experience appear to be more intense than the other two. So, the Covenant Code

---

181 Assyrian Empire was strong during 9th century (883-824 BCE) and in the latter part of the 8th century (745-727 BCE). In between these two periods, the Assyrian power became weak (783-745 BCE). Probably, Israel witnessed the rise and falls of the Assyrian Empire and modified the legislation.

that was codified under the Assyrian colonial times in Israel exhibit a rather more oppressive feature than the other two. This is particularly seen in the way women are treated in these three law codes. The treatment of women in the Covenant code is comparatively more degrading than the Deuteronomic and the Holiness Code. I argue that this is because of the particular degrading colonial experience and the collaborative Israelite elements who supported the colonialism may perhaps be behind the composition or the codification of this law code. In this law code women are degraded. I argue that not only patriarchy but also the colonial ideology led to this phenomenon.

The writer uses subaltern reading because in a colonial context the women of the colonists also turn out to be oppressors. So, the women of the subjected population experience a kind of double subjugation not only from the male colonists and the native men but also from the female colonists. A general feminist approach therefore is not useful in analyzing this specific experience of the colonized subject women population.

The final observation is about the position of women in India. This section will highlight briefly the position of women in religion and society. It will ascertain whether the position of women in India falls in line with the position of women in AWA.

Conclusion

The purpose of God, the creator, who created humankind (male and female) in His image, was to treat both sex as equal partners but in the course of time, Israel got influenced by her neighboring nations, and competed with them by borrowing their culture and practices. Wealth and productivity of the land became a target against women. The same situation can be seen worldwide. The psychological, social, cultural and religious differences between men and women, which are a construct and preponderance of patriarchy and colonial power/s, must be relooked. Therefore, these insights from the Hebrew Bible should be helpful in understanding the milieu.

God is the one who subverts all that marginalizes the people irrespective of their class, color or gender and subverts imperialistic power. God who curtailed the power of Pharaoh over Israel expects the people of Israel to serve each other but unfortunately the laws in Exodus support the vested interest of those who subvert the marginalized. When we compare the Deuteronomic Code with the Book of the Covenant Code, we learn that the Deuteronomic code favors the whole strata of society irrespective of who they are. The most remarkable and unique feature of the Deuteronomic Code is its deep concern for the welfare of all individuals irrespective of class and gender. For Deuteronomy justice is not to be administered solely in accordance with his/her position or voice in the community/society, rather it is concerned with every individual according to his/her need. The laws in Deuteronomy safeguard the poor, weak, marginalized and the defenseless. There is no separation of freedom and welfare based on class and gender. The revolution of freedom, equality and justice for all is one of the prominent threads in Deuteronomic legislation.

Chapter 2

Kingship in Israel: Power Play behind the Traditions

Introduction

The emergence of kingship in Israel is ambiguous as there are passages supporting and negating the institution of kingship.[182] The institution of kingship in Israel is of great importance as it brought Israel in par with her neighboring nations. When the elders of Israel demanded for a king (I Samuel 8), Samuel being a judge opposed out rightly. The unhealthy request among the elders/covenant people resulted in appointing the king. Samuel with much hesitant appointed Saul not as a *melek* (king) but as *nagid* (translated as 'prince', 'leader' or 'commander'). In due course, he was removed[183] and was replaced by David as king. Saul was a Yahwist. He committed mistake and was removed from the throne and his descendants were barred from

[182] The passages that support kingship are found in Judges 17:6, 18:1, 19:1, 21:25, I Sam 9:1-10:16, 11:1-15 and the passages unfavorable to kingship are in I Sam 8:5ff, 10:17-27 and 12:1-25.

[183] The text points out the removal of Saul due to disobedience (e.g. I Sam 15).

the throne. David also a Yahwist was appointed as king. He too committed sin but his confession made him and his descendants to remain in the throne.[184] It is argued that Samuel and David (Levitical and Judahite tradition) played the active role in the Israelite society and Saul (Benjamite) a passive role.

The pertinent questions need to be addressed are: Are traditions in creative tension? Was there any form of power play behind the traditions? Why David was honored and Saul rejected, dishonored and replaced? Why the narrator highlighted Saul in a pessimistic way and David highly placed? Does David's appointment as king has to do with Genesis chapter 49 where Judah was promised for kingship (vv.8-12)? Whether Samuel's displeasure towards kingship has to do with Ancient West Asian borrowing of kingship, where kingship was equated with divine position? All these are relevant questions which penetrates the mind of the inquisitive readers. It will be difficult to address all these questions in this chapter, but it will of course stimulate the readers for further research.

This chapter is an attempt to re-visit the Israelite kingship against the background of Ancient West Asian kingship focusing mainly on kingship of Saul and the power play of dominant traditions.

Ancient West Asian Understanding of Kingship

Kingship was the foundation of civilized life in the great cultures of the Ancient West Asia. Security, peace and justice could not prevail without a ruler to guide them. The kings stood at the center of religious realm in Ancient West Asian cultures, because sacred and secular powers were considered to derive from divine mandate and to be intimately related. The king provided the vital contact between the world below and the world above. Human society was viewed as integral part of the large cosmos, and it was the king's function to maintain the harmony of that assimilation. It was precisely the kings'

[184] David committed sin but texts indicate his repentance (e.g. Psalm 51).

function to maintain the harmony. However, the precise concept of kingship varied extensively within specific cultural contexts.[185]

Egypt

Egyptian kingship appeared at the close of the pre-dynastic period. The customary Egyptian word for king is king of Upper and Lower Egypt. Other words include Ruler, Lord, and Lord of the two lands.[186] According to the Egyptian understanding, the living king is both man and God, and only when he is dead he becomes God. He alone is authorized to communicate with the gods. The king was truly the sole source of authority. All official actions, both in the secular and in the religious sphere were controlled and authorized by the king. In principle, he alone was entitled to carry out the daily ritual of the cult, although in practice he entrusted it to the whole class of the priests.[187]

An Egyptian king was conceived of as a divine being actually descended from the gods. Although living among mortals, he remained an important part of the divine world, a continual

---

[185] Eric M. Meyers and John Rogerson, "Law in ANE and Israel", *The Cambridge Companion to the Bible*, Ed. Bruce Chilton, (The Cambridge University Press, 1997), 138.

[186] Helmer Ringgren, "Understanding of Kingship in the Ancient West Asia", *TDOT*, Vol. 8, Ed. G. Johannes Butter Weck, (UK: William B. Eerdmans Publishing Company, 1997), 349. According to Helmer Ringgren, from the very beginning of Egyptian history, the king was identified in the written sources with Horus- 'the Lofty one'. The earliest kings link the term Horus with the individual name of the ruler. During the enthronement ceremony, the king receives the royal protocol with the five royal names designating him as Horus, Horus of Gold and as the Son of Re. As Horus he is the legitimate heir to the throne, following his deceased father, who has become Osiris. As king of Upper and Lower Egypt, he embodies in his own person the unity of the two halves of the empire. As Son of Re, he represents the sun god and creator who made and maintains the cosmic order. He represents the latter also in the verbal expression 'appear'. Just as the primeval god appeared at the beginning and created the world, and just as Re appears each morning, so also does the king appears on his throne and create order in the Land. The ceremonial act of coronation indicate that a new kind of being had been born. It raised the divinity of the king into the state of 'becoming'.

[187] Siegfried Morenz, *Egyptian Religion,* translated by Ann E. Keep, (London: Methuen & Co. Ltd., 1973), 37-40.

reincarnation of the god Horus, who lived in mysterious communion with his predecessor, Osiris. The rulers were attributed superhuman physical powers qualities characteristics only of the gods. They enjoyed a status that embodied the community's freedom from fear and uncertainty.[188] The king is thus god and the son of a god but is so only by virtue of his office otherwise he is a human being with human characteristics. The king's task is to 'make the land flourish again as it did in primeval times by the plans of Maat (daughter of Sun god Re). In this respect he embodies the creator god. Just as the creator god through command and wisdom, made the world and Maat ruling in it, so also is it said of the king. '*Hu* (Authoritative utterance) is in your mouth, *Sia* (understanding) in your heart, your speech is the shrine of the *Maat* (truth)" Just as the creator was lone at the beginning, so also does the king vanquish his enemies alone (e.g. Ramases II at the battle of Kadesh).[189]

The king is also considered as the shepherd of his people and is to care for them just as a shepherd does for his flock. An effective reign of a king also enhances the fruitfulness of nature. Thus, new kings are greeted as the bringers of a time of salvation with rich harvests, good fortune, and joy throughout the land. The king as ruler is responsible for the establishment and maintenance of temples.[190]

In short, king in Egypt is considered as god dwelling among humankind. The king exercises his authority over humankind and the people are expected to follow the words of the king.

Mesopotamia

In Mesopotamia, like Egypt, kingship emerged at the beginning of historical times. The oldest political institution was the assembly of all free men, i.e., elders. The elders were the influential members of the community and the head of the families. They were designated in Sumerian by the word "*abba*", i.e., father. The power to deal current matters was in the hands of a group of elders, and in the time of emergency they chose a king to take charge for a limited

188 Eric M. Meyers and John Rogerson, "Law in ANE and Israel", 1997, 139.

189 Helmer Ringgren, "Understanding of Kingship in the Ancient West Asia," 349.

190 Helmer Ringgren, "Understanding of Kingship in the Ancient West Asia."

period. Mesopotamian kingship was introduced to meet emergencies with which the existing organs of government were unable to cope. So, when danger comes, the assembly elected a king to whom they delegate power. His power would not outlast the emergency. This structure is absent in Egypt.[191]

The Mesopotamian culture lacked coherence. In Mesopotamian cultures, the concept of the divine essence and the status of the monarch which was fundamental to Egyptian culture and religion were not developed. Kings were considered as mortal endowed with a divine burden. The Mesopotamian word for 'king' is '*lugal*' literally means 'great man'. Although, the king was a heroic person and leader of his people, he was not essentially different from his fellows. Mesopotamian rulers were elected by the gods, but they did not necessarily enjoy the benefit of special divine counsel. They were made to carry a superhuman charge and the gods can remove him at any time and can bestow it upon another. Kings and commoners alike were forced to seek knowledge from rites, dreams and omens in order to perform their respective duties in accordance with the often impulsive will of the gods. The kings in Mesopotamia served three functions: 1. Administer the realm faithfully, 2. Represent the people prayerfully before the gods to ensure prosperity and well-being and 3. Serve the gods regularly by building temples for them and by officiating at their state festivals.[192]

The society and nature were not as seamlessly integrated in Mesopotamia as they were in Egyptian ideology. The harmony between the world of the gods and the world of the human kind was by no means assured. Since the ruler was himself only a mortal, he was stood anxious before the unpredictable will of the gods. As a consequence of this lack of divine status, in Mesopotamia the community maintained considerable independence from the king.[193]

---

[191] Henri Frankfort, *Kingship and the Gods: A Study of Ancient Near Eastern Religion as the integration of society and nature*, (Chicago: The University of Chicago press, 1965), 215.

[192] Eric M. Meyers and John Rogerson, "Law in ANE and Israel," 139.

[193] Eric M. Meyers and John Rogerson, "Law in ANE and Israel."

Kingship in Ancient West Asia: A Comparison

Though kingship is the basis of civilization in Ancient West Asia, yet we find a contrast between the two main centers of ancient civilization. Egypt and Mesopotamia held very different views with regard to the nature of the king. The Mesopotamian king was charged with maintaining harmonious relations between human society and the supernatural powers, yet he was considered as a member of the community. The king is a 'great man'. The king was appointed by the elders and the source of authority purely lies in his election by the assembly of the elders. In Egypt, unlike Mesopotamia was considered as god, i.e., god had descended among men. Pharaoh was not mortal but god. Pharaoh was of divine essence, a god incarnate. In this respect there is a complete contrast.[194] In Mesopotamia, the great power assigned to a king was only for a shorter period of time, which is not so in the case of Egyptian king. The significance of this divergence is very clear. In Egypt the community has freed itself from fear and uncertainty by considering its king as a god whereas in Mesopotamia the community has considerable independence, since its ruler was a man.

The nation Israel is placed geographically between Mesopotamia and Egypt. The history is clear in pointing out that the Hebrew people/Israel lived in Egypt and Mesopotamia for a longer period of time. The pertinent question here arises is: Was the institution of kingship in Israel a fusion of these neighboring nations?

Israelite Understanding Towards Kingship

Kingship as mentioned above is an old and well established phenomenon in Egypt and Mesopotamia, but it is new, foreign, problematic, challenging and dangerous for the newly founded nation Israel. For Israel, covenant was central and kingship was a new order misbalancing the entire structure of Israelite society.

The fusion of Egyptian and Mesopotamian understanding of kingship is seen in the institution of kingship in Israel. The Israelite kingship instead of portraying the king as god or son of god addresses

---

[194] Henri Frankfort, *Kingship and the Gods: A Study of Ancient Near Eastern Religion as the integration of society and nature*, 215.

it as divine election (I Samuel 10:24; 16:1; Deut. 17:15 etc.). However, outside the historical books, the king is depicted as 'son' of God but in a purely figurative way (Psalm 2:7).[195] The conception that the king became a 'son' to Yahweh (Psalm 2:7) may reflect the royal ideology of the Canaanites, who also referred to their monarch in this way, mediating between the Egyptian and Mesopotamian models.

In Ancient West Asia, the king was the head of the cult, which is not so in the case of Israel. In Egypt, the cultic duties were performed by the priests but as an agent of Pharaoh. In Mesopotamia, the king has the title of priest. It was king's responsibility to maintain the temples and its cultic order. However, Israel's monarchy is grounded not on priesthood. They had the right to perform altar service and were charged with the maintenance of altars and temples, but they never earn the title 'priest', and their priestly function was a by-role.[196] When King Saul performed sacrifice, he was ridiculed by Samuel and paid the price by losing the office of king.

Traditional Differences in the Understanding of Kingship

The understanding of kingship differs within the Hebrew Bible, which is a creative tension. We could locate two traditions in the Hebrew Bible: Deuteronomistic tradition and Chronicler tradition.

Deuteronomistic Understanding towards Kingship

Deuteronomic tradition is the powerful tradition of Levitical priesthood originating in the Northern Kingdom. Deuteronomistic traditions consider the Israelite monarchy as alien institutions which represent a decisive break with what had gone before. This social change operates independently of previous social structures. As far as social-cultural factors during the kingship period are concerned, both positive and negative impacts were already existed towards the final phase of the tribal confederation. The writings of the

---

[195] Yehezkel Kaufmann, *The Religion of Israel: From its Beginnings to the Babylonian Exile*, (London: George Allen & Unwin Ltd., 1960), 266.

[196] Yehezkel Kaufmann, *The Religion of Israel: From its Beginnings to the Babylonian Exile.*

Deuteronomistic history reflect the shared norms and values, beliefs and attitude of the community which the author (Samuel) belongs.[197]

Gerhard von Rad proposes the theory that the Deuteronomistic tradition had roots in northern Israelite religion and was brought to Judah and cultivated there by rural Levitical priest who set themselves the task of awakening the spirit of the old religion of Yahweh. This priestly circle produced Deuteronomy history around the time of Josiah to keep alive the old northern tradition in which they stood and to make this tradition applicable to their own historical situation.[198]

Hence, in Deuteronomistic history we can see the role of Northern and prophetic circle. They traced their root to Samuel, and it found in Saul as illustrative model of all that was wrong-headed in Israel's kings. Samuel, the local seer becomes for them the dominant figure and opponent of Saul (I Samuel 9:1-10:16. 10:17-25, 12; 13:8-15). Saul's suffering and death becomes just the fate expected for one who would take over the sovereignty of Samuel's God.[199]

Chronicler Understanding towards Kingship

Chronicler unlike Deuteronomistic understanding is positive towards Davidic kingship. It exalts David as Yahweh's anointed. It projected David as an ideal figure. In doing so, the narrator omitted unfavorable events in David's life. In Chronicler history the role of Southern and Davidic circle can be seen. They certify David's claims to kingship over Israel though he was the Judean and not the first king. David is presented as the man chosen and supported by Yahweh in the face of all opposition, and this is accepted by seeing him over against the divinely rejected Saul, whose deterioration marks a counterpart to

---

[197] Daniel Jones Muthunayagam, "Cultural Shifts from the Period of Tribal Confederation to Monarchy", *BTF,* Vol.32, (2000), 9.

[198] Patricia Dutcher Walls, "The Social Location of the Deuteronomist: A Sociological study of factional politics in late pre-exilic Judah", *JSOT,* Vol.52, (1991), 79.

[199] W. Lee Humphreys, "The Rise and Fall of King Saul: A Study of Ancient Narrative Stratum in I Samuel" *JSOT,* Vol.18, (1980), 76.

the able and ideal youth who becomes the heroic, ideal future king (I Samuel 17-23, 27:1-28:2, 29-30; II Samuel 1-5).[200]

The book of Chronicles contains an excessive idealization of Davidic dynasty. The Chronicler seems to select materials furthering his own purpose. The Davidic promise and victories are seen as blessings awarded to David for seeking the Lord. Saul's kingship was taken away by the Lord and was killed by the heathen because he neglected the command of God. It appears that the Chronicler selected materials from the life of Saul to serve its purpose. The image of Saul is projected in a negative way (I Chronicles 10). In Chronicler history Saul's head is hung up (I Chronicles 10:10) whereas in Deuteronomistic history, his body is hung (I Samuel 31:10) up. Does this discrepancy have to do with tradition? Why the Chronicler historian used the word 'head' instead of 'body'? In I Samuel 5:1-6, head of the Dagon was cut off and in I Samuel 17, David chopped Goliath's head. It seems Chronicler is conveying a strong message to his readers that Saul like Dagon and Goliath is God's enemy and he faced the same fate. The Chronicler's intention is to exalt David as an ideal person and as a king of promise. The Chronicler's sees Israel's first king Saul as a figure of disobedience, failure and rejection. The Chronicler history is more interested in Judah rather Benjamite or any other tribe.

In short, the Deuteronomistic tradition places Samuel as the model and the Chronicler's model is David. It seems both traditions place Saul on a darker side in order to project their model.

Observations Based on Kingship in Israel

Kingship: A blessing or a curse?

Throughout Ancient West Asia, kings were regarded as supreme human beings and even receive the divine status. The Egyptian king during the enthronement ceremony receives royal names designating him as Horus and as the son of Re. He represents the creator who made and maintains the cosmic order. The king is thus god and the son of God in virtue of his office. The king's responsibility is to make

[200] W. Lee Humphreys, "The Rise and Fall of King Saul: A Study of Ancient Narrative Stratum in I Samuel", 76.

the land flourish and to be the shepherd of his people. Similarly, the Sumerian king is called as great man who came down from heaven and is thus a divine institution. Enthronement is considered as a symbolic rebirth and receives the status of a son of God. In Assyria, king was considered as great man. In Babylon too king was considered as supreme and receives the divine epithet as god or Lord. In short, in almost all religion and cultures of Ancient West Asia, king was highly placed.

Does Samuel and the prophetic tradition from which Deuteronomistic historiography came into existence was afraid of such trends? There is a possibility as Samuel made it clear in I Samuel 8:11-17 about the ways of the king. How he came to know about the ways or rights of the king? Definitely Samuel being a judge for years was well acquainted about the nature and functioning of the kings of the neighboring nations. So, Samuel and the prophetic traditions in order to keep their traditions alive considered kingship as danger, but the elders who observed the threatening, well-being and safety of their wealth considered it as a necessity by which they can compete with their neighboring nations and protect their interests.

Traditions in conflict: Old order (Judge) or New order (Kingship)?

The kingship accounts particularly I Samuel 8-12 make it ample clear that certain ardent followers of Yahweh perceived kingship as a dangerous one. On the other hand, there was a group who apparently considered it as a new shift of prosperity both politically and economically, as they thought that the kingship will make her stable like her neighboring nations and her wealth will boost and they will be safe. A creative tension can be seen between these two groups and the one who was having upper hand in the community dominated the scene. In these chapters we can see mainly three traditions out of which two dominated and the third one suffered greatly. The book of Samuel was dominated initially by the prophetic circles who considered Samuel as close to God and a chosen leader. It was Samuel who exercised the authority in every matters of the society whether it is political, economic, social and religious. This tradition replaced the priestly group of Eli and dominated the scene. When they faced challenges by the elders of the community in chapter 8, through judgmental words tried to dominate and control the repulsive voice. In course of time, a shift took place. The royal Davidic dynasty came to the scene and took over the mantle from the prophetic traditions. If we read carefully the prophetic groups' role was visible during the time of Eli and particularly in the time of Saul but started weakening in the rule of David. Saul played only a passive role although like David he too was anointed and appointed by Yahweh. It is very interesting to note that Samuel's role representing prophetic circle starts from chapter 2 and continued throughout the rule of Saul and slowed down in the time of David, and on the other hand, the role of David appear in the scene from chapter 15 (when Saul disobeyed, the word came clearly that "The Lord has torn the kingdom of Israel from you this very day, and has given it to a neighbor of yours, who is better than you" I Samuel 15:28). Does this change of guard have anything to do with the blessings of Jacob given to Judah and Benjamin (Genesis 49:8-12, 27)? There is a possibility. The third group, the Benjamite-Saulide dynasty/margin was hard-pressed and trapped between the two dominant traditions/centers. Here comes the creative tension: Whether Saul was placed to replace and whether he was displaced by the dominant traditions.

Saul: Placed to Displace?

Saul seems to serve as an illustration of all that was perverse in kingship from the perspective of Samuel and prophetic circles.[201] This can be seen right from his selection to his dethronement. He is first portrayed as an innocent and incompetent leader and finally as a villain. Saul's unfitness to lead the people of Israel is foreshadowed in the opening narrative. In chapter 9 Saul is depicted as a weak shepherd. Saul though was living within 5 miles from the territory of Samuel, yet completely ignorant of the most significant spiritual figure since Moses.[202] He is projected as a tall man. Does his stature

[201] W. Lee Humphreys, "The rise and fall of King Saul: A Study of ancient narrative stratum in I Samuel", 75.

[202] Robert D. Bergen, "I and II Samuel", 113.

is compared with Goliath? The text is not clear. When God asked Samuel to appoint Saul as *nagid,* why Samuel secretly anointed Saul rather than in public at least before the invitees and Saul's servant (I Samuel 9:27-10:1)? The text is not stating. Possibly he was not happy and anointed him secretly to give a low profile to him and continue to have an upper hand.

The lot casting ceremony through which an individual is selected out from a larger group requires Saul's presence; however the narrator informs us that he was hiding among the baggage. If he was chosen and anointed (ch.9), why again a lot casting was needed? This also shows a sign of healthy discontentment within Samuel and the prophetical circles.

In the Ammonite war once again Saul was renewed as king? Why again a renewal needed, if he was anointed and then chosen by lot? The prophetic circle in order to project Samuel and his supremacy over Saul perhaps inserted 'Samuel' in the scene. There is a discrepancy in vv.12-14. After the victory, the people asked Samuel, "who is it that said, 'Shall Saul reign over us?' Give them to us so that we may put to death." Samuel is silent and the response comes from Saul. Why is it so? In verse 14, Samuel said to the people, "Come let us go to Gilgal and there renew the kingship." Why again a renewal needed? There is a secondary insertion most probably from the prophetic circles.

The connections between chapters 11 and 12 seem to be a redactor's job rather than a historical sequence. Saul is not at all mentioned in this pericope and in verse 12 the reason behind the demand of a king is King Nahash of Ammonite which is not mentioned or hinted in chapter 8. Moreover in chapter 11 the victory over the Ammonite was credited as positive but here the Ammonite crisis led to a sinful demand for a king, which is a clear picture that it is not from same source. In chapter 12 once again Samuel is defending his position by vindicating himself first and then God and pointing the king. It is very interesting to note that Samuel was not happy of kingship and God though not pleased but agreed and finally chosen and anointed Saul. But in verse 13, Samuel states, 'here is the king whom you have chosen'. Finally Samuel adopted a strange method, a thunder and rain in an unusual time. This made the people to fear Samuel and God and made them to repent from their sin.

This incident paved way for the rejection and removal of Saul. If we observe carefully, Saul's rejection in chapter 13 and 15 took place in Gilgal. According to 10:8, Saul a young man was supposed to wait in Gilgal for Samuel and for 7 days, but the incident of chapter 13 seem to be conducted by Saul having a grown up son Jonathan who is capable for war. This clearly shows that the narrator inserted Gilgal to picture Saul as a disobedient king. In chapter 15, Saul once again was pointed for his sinful activity and though he accepted his mistake and begged for forgiveness but Samuel passed out strong word against Samuel. As Samuel began to leave, Saul grabbed Samuel's robe and it tore. Grasping the hem was the final act of supplication on Saul's part but Samuel took it as a sign of Saul's removal from the throne (15: 27-28).The text says that "The Lord has torn the kingdom of Israel from you this very day, and has given it to a neighbors of yours, who is better than you". Whom the narrator is pointing? If it is David, the question arises, whether David was better than Saul. The text says, Saul was removed from the throne and replaced by David. Saul a Yahwist committed lesser crime and was removed and David also a Yahwist made a gross mistake but continued on the throne. Taking all this development into account, there is a possibility that both 13:7b-15a and 15:1-35 have been shaped by the prophetic circles to prepare the way for David, to communicate a strong message to the reader that the people's demand led to failure and also to send a message to the wider audience that prophets had an upper hand in the overall functioning of the society. In short, Saul was placed to be replaced and displaced. The story of Saul was a preparation for David. Tradition played the key role.

Conclusion

The issue of kingship as such seems to be ambiguous. It was part of God's plan, but the people of Israel adopted a wrong method, which finally brought them into a situation of exile. To make it more clear, the issue in the texts as such is not against kingship but a proper kingship in which God could exercise His Sovereignty and could have His control over His people. There are plenty of examples like

King Josiah and Jehoshaphat who excelled in their responsibility by surrendering to the will of God and people of Israel had a peaceful time under their leadership.

If we take the Old Testament as a whole, a common thread is visible, which passes throughout, and takes a small beginning or a small person to a larger picture. For instance, Israel as a tiny nation originally of nomads becomes a great nation. Saul, a Benjamite, from the smallest tribe exhibited charismatic power; and David though from the tribe of Judah was ignored from his family but later brought fame and glory to the nation. All these incidences projects a picture that Israel in their daily life paid due reverence to God. God was not against kingship, but unhappy with the attitude and motivation of His people which resulted in division and exile.

Hence, the picture of both monarchy and anti-monarchy reflects the tension and power play between the traditions. This tension gripped the life of Israel. Though the demand of Israel prevailed over the words of Samuel and God, but in the course of time it deteriorated and finally resulted into shame (division and exile).

The newly created Israelite nation directly or indirectly was influenced by the belief, faith and customs of Ancient West Asia. History and tradition of Ancient West Asia played a crucial role in the shaping of Israelite history and tradition. The influence was not only one of critical in political, social, economic and religious change, but also literary and theological experimentation. In response to such influence, periods of change and radical shift occurred in Israelite history resulting in new forms. The history of Israel was not a stagnant one rather a flowing one, which shaped and reshaped in the courses of her history. Lot of shifts and changes happened in Israelite history. The kingship issue was one of those changes. It was a common phenomenon in Ancient West Asia but seems a disturbing one for the Israelite who considered herself as unique and had special relationship with Yahweh (covenant community).

Chapter 3

Ruth, the Outsider and Naomi, the Insider

Introduction

Creating a space to have an identity is considered as success. In order to have an identity, people long to do something different in life. In Bible there are scores of characters who created an identity in foreign lands. They are Joseph and Moses in Egypt, Daniel in Babylon, Nehemiah and Esther in Persia and Ruth in the land of Israel. A careful observation reveals that they all faced stiff challenges and opposition to create a mark in history. It is quite interesting to learn that apart from Ruth almost all characters had support of a few in their road to success. Ruth was different from all these characters. Ruth was in a triple disadvantage position. She is a Moabite/Gentile, woman and a widow. Her identity is not a promising one in the eyes of a Jewish ethnic and Patriarchal world.

This chapter is an attempt to explore the role of a marginalized gentile woman in a world of Jewish ethnic and patriarchal dominated center. The pertinent questions to be addressed are: Does Ruth's decision to migrate from Moab to Bethlehem was to confute her land, culture and religion to identify with the people of other faith?

Is it merely a love and loyalty of daughter-in-law towards mother-in-law or points out an alternative/inclusive community where margin and center live together?

Book of Ruth: A Brief Overview

The book begins with the tragedy of a Jewish family that left the land of Bethlehem 'House of Bread' to a land of Moab 'from my father' and ends with a generous broad minded liberal Jew 'Boaz' representing the center who is receptive to a woman of other faith 'Ruth, the Moabite' representing the margin[203] The movement of Elimelech from Bethlehem to Moab ends with a disaster and the movement of Ruth from Moab to Bethlehem ends up with a blessing. Recently few scholars such as Laura E. Donaldson,[204] Moshe J. Bernstein[205] and others highly praised Orpah for her strong determination to be in her land, religion and culture. In the context of such an alternative readings, a fresh reading of the book of Ruth is essential to shed light on the neglected portrayal of Ruth, the Moabite.

The opening verse of Ruth sets the time 'in the days when the judges ruled.' Based on this reference we can arrive with a possible conclusion that this book was written between 1380 and 1050 BCE. The days of judges were a period of political, religious and social anarchy (Judges 21:25). During this period, the famine made Elimelech and his family to migrate to the land of Moab for survival. However, the migration from Bethlehem to Moab ended up in tragedy, i.e., losing all male members in the family, thereby

---

[203] Shiju Mathew, 'Ruth, a Moabite Gentile Woman Blessing the Nation Israel: A Subaltern Reading,' New Life Theological Journal 3/2, 2013, 69; Shiju Mathew, 'Ruth: The Immigrant, a Journey from Moab to Bethlehem,' in *Re-imagining Reformation: Essays in Honor of P. G. George*, ed. Y.T. Vinayaraj, Dexter Maben, Woba James (Delhi: ISPCK, 2017), 224.

[204] Laura E. Donaldson, "The sign of Orpah: Reading through native eyes", *Vernacular Hermeneutics,* R. S. Sugirtharajah (ed.), (Sheffield: Sheffield Academic Press, 1999).

[205] Bernstein, Moshe J, "Two Multivalent readings in the Ruth narrative", *JSOT* 50 (1991), 15-26.

resulting to three women in men's world. Naomi decided to return[206] to her place of birth leaving back the two widowed daughter-in-law. After much persuasion of Naomi, Orpah decided to be in her land, culture and religion. Ruth though proud of her land, culture and religion decided to migrate to the land of strangers that shows her devotion to her aged mother-in-law and also to the God of her mother-in-law. Her decision and determination resulted into a rich dividend. Her future though bleak knowing the stigma of being a widow and Moabite, the life blooms into graceful human love story, a reenactment of Covenant God's love for His chosen people. Moreover, the movement gradually blessed her generation towards royal lineage (David) and messianic lineage (Jesus). In short, the movement of Elimelech ended up in disaster whereas the movement of Ruth is rewarded with great blessings from God.

The book of Ruth is well structured and is in a symmetrical design. We can bring out four main episodes.

First episode: Naomi's hardship

Second episode: Ruth's love and loyalty towards her widowed mother-in-law

Third episode: Boaz's generosity and kindness towards the widowed Moabites Ruth

Fourth episode: Naomi's comfort and contentment

The Book of Ruth is written by a Jewish author. Hence, a rereading from margin perspective is necessary to shed light on Ruth, the Moabite.

Subaltern Reading of Ruth, the Immigrant

Two out of 39 books in the Hebrew Bible are named after women. Ruth was a gentile mobaite woman who migrated and married a Hebrew man Boaz and Esther was a Hebrew woman who married a gentile king. God used both of them in a strategic time in the history of Israel to preserve the nation. Both books give inclination towards the female experience of struggles in male dominated society and in

---

[206] The word 'return' is a key word and is used more than ten times in the original Hebrew (refer Santha Kumari Mondithoka, 'Ruth,' in *South Asia Bible Commentary*, Brian Wintle (ed.), Udaipur: Open Door Publications, 2015, 333).

spite of male structured society they convey/portray the important role of women and their voices.

Although, the book of Ruth is very small comparing to other historical books, it is appealing and attractive. This book is affiliated with the struggles of common people who live in a world dominated by the elites. It started with tragedy but ended up in victory.

The author has selected a few passages from the book of Ruth which specifically talk about Ruth's identity, her status, potentials and role in lifting her voice to/in a male centered society. Though all the three women Naomi, Ruth and Orpah were bound religiously and within the socio-cultural bindings, they make autonomous choices, which make clear that they are not, dependent on someone else's authority. Ruth in particular steps into a critical juncture in the life of a Jewish family and brings about a positive turn in events, which were proceeding to a troublesome direction. Ruth went ahead of her socio-cultural boundary.

Journey of Elimelech towards Moab: (Ruth 1:3-5)

Elimelech makes a movement from Bethlehem to Moab, a place known as house of Bread to a place ending up in death thereby resulting emptiness in the life of Naomi. After few years Naomi lost her two sons adding more woes in her life. Naomi known as pleasant is left with two Moabite daughter-in-law which is not a welcome sign in the proud Jewish patriarchal set up. As famine shattered the solidarity between the humankind and land, now death destroyed the family. A careful word choice *shaer* (Niphal form) adds poignancy to the verse (v. 3). In the Old Testament, this verb commonly describes bereavement at death (Genesis 7:23; 14:10; 42:38; Exod. 14:28 etc.). This shifts from "his sons" (vv. 1-2) to "her sons" in verse 3 signals a shift of parental claim and responsibility from the dead father to the living mother.[207] NRSV says that Naomi's son 'took', an expression used elsewhere only in postexilic books (Ezra 2:61; 10:10, 14, 17, 18, 44; Nehemiah 6:18, 7:63; 13:23). The term 'took' in verse 4 is used only nine times in the Old Testament to refer marriage (Judges

[207] Phyllis Trible, "Two women in a Man' world: A reading of the Book of Ruth", *Soundings*, 59 (1976), 252-279.

21:23 [reminding us once again the links between the beginning of Ruth and the end of Judges]; in Ezra 9:2, 12; 10:44 and Nehemiah 13:25 [Where the taking of foreign wives is condemned]; and in II Chronicles 11:21; 13:21; 24:3 [in reference to the taking of multiple wives].)[208] It seems the narrator is conveying the message of consequences by marrying heathen women. No satisfactory explanation for either of the wives' names has been proposed. Orpah is usually derived from *Orep,* which means 'back to the neck', i.e., stiff necked. It has also been linked to 'mane', 'cloud', 'perfume', 'aroma', 'kindness' or 'a handful of water'. Ruth is traditionally derived from *raeah*, which means 'friend' or 'friendship'. It also carries the meaning *rawah* which means 'to water abundantly' or 'to be saturated.'[209]

When they had lived about ten years conveys the idea that they lived in Moab about ten years, rather than the idea that they were married for ten years. So, the text is not stating how long they lived after their marriage. If stayed for more than a year, there would have been a possibility for a child. The immediate death brings out a possible judgment of God towards Elimelech and Naomi for their alliance with Moabite. Now, if we read other way, then having no child for both son and for ten years can be considered as a judgment from God. The latter part says that Ruth had son with Boaz. In that case, the mistake lies in the side of Mahlon and Chilion for marrying a woman of other faith. In verse 5, the narrator uses an idiomatic expression 'to be left from' in a unique sense. The use of 'sons' is used explicitly for married men only here in the Old Testament. Though no cause of death is stated in this passage, the Talmud regards it as a punishment for leaving Judah.[210] Though Talmud brings out a judgment for leaving Judah, but it carries a message more than leaving Judah. It brings out a judgment of intermarriage particularly with Moabite. The word of Naomi regarding God in 1:13 and 20-21 supports it. Ruth, the Moabite probably sensing the situation takes up the challenge and enters into an unlikely alliance with Boaz which

---

[208] Leander E. Keck (ed.), "The Book of Ruth", *TNIB*, Vol. 2 (Nashville: Abingdon Press, 1988), 901.

[209] F. B. Huey, "Ruth", 520.

[210] Kirsten Neilson, *Ruth: A Commentary* (Louisville: John Knox Press, 1997), 44.

led Naomi to the path of blessing, the women of Jerusalem praised Naomi.

Journey of Ruth towards Bethlehem: (Ruth 1:14-18; 2:2-7 and 4:11-15)

The journey of Ruth towards Bethlehem was not an easy one knowing the fact that she will not be welcomed by the people of Bethlehem. Perhaps Naomi too had that in mind. Naomi persuaded the maximum to discourage both Orpah and Ruth. Her persuasion yielded result partially when Orpah decided to go back to her people, culture and religion. Ruth had something different in mind. Ruth 1: 14 say, *"Then they (Orpah and Ruth) wept aloud again. Orpah kissed her mother-in-law, but Ruth clung to her."* The verb used in this verse is 'cling' which can also be referred as a marriage relationship (c.f. Genesis 2:24; I Kings 11:2), or to Israel's ideal relationship with God (c.f. Joshua 22:5). In either case, it brings out a picture that Ruth is clinging to Naomi as a male clings to a female or as a devotee to a God. It brings out a message "concern for the 'other'". It shows the role of dedifferentiation. She will not play merely the role of a daughter-in-law rather the role of a son. In other words, what a male can do, she too can do it. Her role of dedifferentiation can be seen from the following chapters.

Naomi tried to take one more chance to change the decision of Ruth. *So she said, see, your sister-in-law has gone back to her people and to her gods; return after your sister-in-law (1:15).*" Naomi appealed subtly to bring pressure, hoping perhaps that a wavering will lurk behind Ruth's form embrace. She quietly tempted Ruth by reminding her people and her gods (national and religious root).[211] Ruth though sensed her culture and religion yet resisted against the temptation by sticking to Naomi. Ruth said, *"Do not press me to leave you or to turn back from following you! Where you go, I will go; where you lodge, I will lodge; your people shall be my people and your God my God (1:16)".* The word 'leave' in this verse frequently connotes 'changing primary allegiance' as in Genesis 2:24, which uses both

[211] Robert L. Hubbard, "The Book of Ruth", *The New International commentary of the Old Testament* (Michigan: Grand Rapids, 1988), 116.

'cling to' and 'to leave.'[212] Ruth's commitment was not limited to the journey back to Bethlehem but was committed to share Naomi's land, culture and religion. The word employed in this verse, brings out a point that Ruth left her land, culture and religion and adopted Naomi's land, culture and religion.

Ruth even further by saying that: *"Where you die, I will die- there I will be buried. May the Lord do this and so to me, and more as well, if even death parts me from you (1:17)."* The oath formula used is found elsewhere in the Old Testament (I kings 19:2), but only in I Samuel 20:13 and in this verse the word '*Yahweh*' is employed rather than the word '*Elohim*'. Ruth though a heathen employs the personal name of God instead of a general term, which once again shows the closer affinity of Ruth towards the belief and practices of Jews.

The emphatic decision of Ruth made Naomi to stop further persuasion. Ruth1:18: *"When Naomi saw that she was determined to go with her, she said no more to her."* Naomi realized the determination of her daughter-in-law and resolved not to argue further. The solemnity of Ruth's curse was itself sufficient to prevent Naomi from further protestations.[213]

Ruth was extraordinarily confident and courageous woman, who participated actively in shaping her own destiny though she faced difficult situations. She had such great love and respect for her Jewish mother-in-law, Naomi that she was willing to live her land, culture and religion. Ruth sacrificed her destiny to 'cling to' an aged, hopeless mother-in-law. Ruth's selfless devotion to Naomi perhaps challenged Boaz to respond in a similar fashion. When a son was born to Ruth and Boaz, the women of Jerusalem overcame their prejudice in acclaiming that Ruth the Moabite was 'better than seven sons.'[214] The weighty question arises from this text is: What forced Ruth to follow a different line followed by Orpah? What was her intention for clinging Naomi? Whether Ruth was challenging the orthodox set pattern of rule exercised by the Jews of her time?

---

[212] Ilona Rashkow, "Ruth: The discourse of power and the power of discourse", in *A Feminist Companion to Ruth*, Athalya Brenner (ed.), (Sheffield: Sheffield Academic press, 1993), 31.

[213] F. B. Huey, "Ruth", 524.

[214] Kwok Pui-lan, *Introducing Asian Feminist Theology*, 57-58.

The whole story of Ruth's challenge and its development centers around 1:16-17, "*Do not press me to leave you or to turn back following you! Where you go, I will go; where you lodge, I will lodge; your people shall be my people and your God my God. Where you die, I will die-there will I be buried. May the Lord do this and so to me, and more as well, if even death parts me from you!*" The motivational force of Ruth's statement and actions is confirmed by Naomi's neighbors to be love stated in 4:15, "....for your daughter-in-law who loves you, who is more to you than seven sons, has borne him". This verse makes Ruth the subject of the single occurrence of the verb 'to love' with Naomi as the direct object.[215] Ruth by joining herself to Naomi willingly joins weakness to weakness and death to death. The rest of the story progresses between these two women. When two women, the outsider and insider joins hand can turn the bitterness to joy, from shadow to reality, from gloom to light.

The unknown author of Ruth continues the story by bringing back Naomi and Ruth, the childless widow from Moab to Bethlehem during the barley season (2:2-7).

After reaching Bethlehem, Ruth decided to take the place of a male member. *She said to Naomi. Let me go to the field and glean among the ears of grain, behind someone in whose sight I may find favor (v.2).* The Hebrew form 'Let me go' is cohortative first person, which means a request for permission or a form determination. There follows the participle regularly described in the grammars as an expression of polite deference a proactive.[216] Ruth's offer meant a readiness to endure more than a hot day's work for small gain. Naomi granted Ruth's request and added an affectionate "my daughter" which is found eight times altogether in the book.[217] *So she went. She came and gleaned in the field behind the reapers. As it happened, she came to the part of the field belonging to Boaz, who was of the family of Elimelech (v. 3).* Is it by chance that Ruth landed in the field of Boaz or whether

[215] Johanna W. H. Boss, "Out of the shadows: Genesis 38; Judges 4:17-22; Ruth 3", *Semeia*, 42 (1988), 58.

[216] Edward F. Campbell Jr. *Ruth,* 91.

[217] F. B. Huey, "Ruth", 527.

Naomi guided her to this field? The text is not clear. However, Ruth a stranger and migrant takes risk to glean the field of a Jewish man.

Just then Boaz came from Bethlehem. He said to the reapers, "The LORD be with you". They answered, "The Lord bless you" (v. 4). The first conversation between Boaz and his workers may reflect a standardized greetings formula. *Then Boaz came*: The string of imperfects with vav-consecutive in verse 3 is interrupted by a clause beginning, an example of a frequent construction in Hebrew narrative style making it "graphic and vivid, and enabling the reader to enter into the surprise of satisfaction of the speaker concerned.[218] *Then Boaz said to his servant who was in charge of the reapers, "To whom does this young woman belong?"* The word *naar* is translated "servant" in vv. 5-6 but the feminine form of the same word *naara* is translated "young woman" in verse 5. The clever storyteller will have some fun with the word throughout the book. Here one must simply observe this emphasis upon youth rather than with servanthood.[219] Boaz asked, to whom does this young woman belong? Obviously, Boaz had noticed Ruth, but what specifically caught his eyes remains uncertain. *The servant who was in charge of the reapers answered, "She is the Moabite who came back with Naomi from the country of Moab (v. 6).* The in-charge of the reapers tells Boaz that Ruth requested to glean and gather the sheaves behind the reapers (v. 7). The meaning of the last part of the speech is not clear. The text can mean either that Ruth has been working in the field since morning or that she has been standing there waiting for Boaz to arrive.[220]

In the culmination of this beautiful piece of story, the protagonist is being eulogized by a heathen woman for her unconditional love and service towards her old, fragile and hopeless mother-in-law. The blessings of Ruth are connected to both Matriarchs (Rachel and Leah) and Tamar. Both Tamar and Ruth took great risks to ensure that the Levirate law was followed. Ruth the Migrant who was a foreigner (*nokriya*), lowest servant (*sipha*),

---

[218] Francis Brown, *The New Brown-Driver-Briggs-Gesenius Hebrew and English Lexicon* (Massachusetts: Hendrickson Publishers, 1977), 244.

[219] Robert L. Hubbard, "The Book of Ruth", 145.

[220] Robert L. Hubbard, "The Book of Ruth", 149-152.

servant (*ama*) became the wife (*issa*) of Boaz 'a man of reputation (4:11-15).'

Then the women said to Naomi, "Blessed be the Lord, who has not left you this day without next-of-kin; and may his name be renowned in Israel. He shall be to you a restorer of life and a nourisher of your old age, for your daughter-in-law who loves you, who is more to you than seven sons, has borne him."(vv. 14-15)" Normally, the naming of the child would immediately follow his birth. Here, however, the author defers that event until verse 17. If men dominated the previous scene (vv. 1-12), this one is for women only.[221] The women of the community who earlier had witnessed Naomi's bitter lament now gathered around her to share her happiness. They praised the Lord, giving him credit for providing a redeemer for Naomi. When the women say that the child is Naomi's redeemer in verse 14, the legally minded may once again belonged to Elimelech. But, the woman of the town defines the child's role in a different way. In their opinion, the child's significance is formulated completely in terms of his meaning for Naomi.[222]

He shall be to you a restorer of life and a nourisher of your old age- The literal force of here is to "restore life", as in Job 33:30. As such it is the transitive (or causative) reflex of the idiom "life returns, is restored," as in a figurative sense, "to revive/restore someone's spirit, courage, or strength" in the sense of restoring a normal, full state of being.[223] The MT's emphatic word order points directly to the child's mother, *your daughter-in-law.* The sudden appearance of this kinship term is very significant. It implies that, though now Boaz's wife, Ruth still enjoyed a familial relationship to Naomi as Mahlon's widow. More importantly, what assured Naomi of the child's care was not social obligation or family ties but Ruth's deep affection to her.[224] Ruth finally received the praise she rightly

---

[221] Phyllis Trible, "Two women in a Man' world: A reading of the Book of Ruth", 277.

[222] F. B. Huey, "Ruth", 546.

[223] Frederic Bush, *Word Biblical Commentary: Ruth and Esther*, vol. 9 (Dallas: Word Books Publishers, 1996), 257.

[224] Robert L. Hubbard, "The Book of Ruth", 272-273.

deserved, as she is compared better than seven sons. The margin won the heart of the center.

Ruth, the Outsider: Identifying and Partnering with the Insiders

1. *Ruth: the Staggering Personality Budding out of the Dimness*

Ruth and Orpah adopted two different paths. Orpah after much persuasion from her mother-in-law decided to remain in her land, religion and culture. Ruth probably knowing the alienation of Israel towards Moab and the judgment meted out to Naomi due to her alliance with Moab decided to stand against the thought pattern. It finally brought blessing to Naomi and in turn to the people of Israel. Ruth challenged the norm of the day. She makes an unlikely alliance with Naomi which continued throughout the narrative. This alliance provides a counter-theme especially to the betrothal alliance and thereby challenges patriarchal values.

2. *Ruth, the Active and Naomi, the Passive*

Naomi faced hardship and instead of taking active role opted for a passive role. Ruth on the other hand faced hardship and though in a foreign land and in a strange culture took an active role. If Naomi was active in chapter 1, Ruth was active in the rest of the book. If the role of Naomi was active to passive, the role of Ruth was passive to active. Why a shift in role? Is it to counter the male dominated mentality, where women are expected to be silent and submissive? Is it due to the male dominated tradition, where the 'others' are ignored and taken in a lighter note? The role of Naomi was from a 'wife' to 'lost woman'. She lost her major roles. She is left with little role to the larger institutions of the society (1:21). If so, Ruth too went through the same fate. She too lost her husband. Her role unlike Naomi was a role of difference, a role of dedifferentiation. When Naomi adopted a silent approach, Ruth took a bold step to silent the male prejudice mind and thinking. A gradual shift can be seen in the role of Ruth. She enters the story in 1:4, where she is named. Her act started from 1:14, when she and Orpah provide different responses to Naomi's role. The crises of death and Naomi's act led directly to her dedifferentiation. Orpah accepts her role as bereaved daughter-in-law and obeys Naomi by returning to her culture. Ruth however, deviates from her mother-in-law's command. She clings to Naomi. When she clings to Naomi, she takes the role of a male member in initiating a relationship of commitment similar to marriage. It was a not a role of replacement rather a role of addition. She continued as a daughter-in-law but also took key role in taking the affair of household activities (chapter 2-3). Her role was not merely a role of daughter-in-law but also a family role of husband, son and a gleaner.[225]

3. *Ruth, the Foreigner Changing the Affluence of Naomi, the Native*

The text clearly reveals that Naomi opted for a silent approach throughout the book and Ruth took the place of her deceased husband and displayed an active role. Orpah left Naomi and Ruth was forced to return to her home. Ruth instead of following Orpah's model surprised Naomi by making an oath of allegiance. Naomi instead of appreciating Ruth surprised Ruth and the readers by silent approach. When Naomi saw that she was determined to go with her, she said no more to her, so the two of them went on until they came to Bethlehem-1:18-19. This is her first silence. When they arrived in Bethlehem, Naomi failed to introduce her daughter-in-law to the women of the town (1:19-22). The strange expression of Naomi is "I went away full, but the Lord has brought me back empty". The presence of Ruth the Moabite is not acknowledged, which is her second silence. The third silence of Naomi is her failure to inform Ruth about her relative Boaz (2:1-3).[226] What is the reason behind her silence? Why she hesitated to take her daughter-in-law to Bethlehem? Why she failed to introduce Ruth to the women of the town? Why she failed to disclose the information of Boaz to Ruth? These questions need further investigation.

[225] Berquist, Jon L, "Role dedifferentiation in the Book of Ruth", *JSOT* 57 (1993), 24-28.

[226] Coxon, Peter W, "Was Naomi a Scold? A response to Fewell and Gunn", *JSOT* 45 (1989), 25-28.

The role of Ruth unlike Naomi was active throughout. She was proud of her culture, but took it as a challenge of her life to follow Naomi, which is clearly stated in 1:16-17. Though Naomi tried to withdraw emotionally from Ruth but her strong determination is highly appreciable. The characterization of Ruth is a remarkable one. She was mentally prepared to defy her social culture and custom in order to overcome the obstacles that stand in her way. She brushed aside the feeling among the Jews that she is a Moabite. This can be seen from chapter 2-3, where Naomi stayed at home and she worked throughout the day in the field. In chapter 1:16-17, she stated her purpose of life and in the following chapters she acted to achieve and fulfill it. This act not only won the approval from Boaz but also the national seal of approval as an Israelite woman (2:11-12). Ruth came out from shadow and entered into the wider Israelite community not by compulsion rather through her action. The narrator at the end makes a remarkable expression. Ruth is no longer a servant or handmaid, but a woman whom the Lord will make like Rachel and Leah, who together built up the house of Israel (4:11-12). The women of the town praise Ruth further by comparing Ruth better than seven sons (4:15). Ruth a stranger changed the fortune of Naomi.

Ruth the Moabite finally turned out to be a blessing and light to Naomi and thereafter to the succeeding generation of Israel.

4. *Ruth, an Important Historical Figure of Israel*

Ruth's movement to Bethlehem with Naomi against the wind was rewarded by becoming a significant part of Israelite political and religious history in the form of a godly king David and messiah Jesus Christ. Her initiative to move to a foreign land draws many other women in the mind of the narrator (Rachel, Leah, Tamar, the women of Bethlehem). The book of Ruth was read at the Jewish feast of Pentecost, which falls seven weeks after the Passover. The reading of the book is a remainder to the covenant community about Yahweh's special favor to those who wholeheartedly embrace the voice of God as Ruth the Moabite did.

It is interesting to note the placement of the book of Ruth in both English and Hebrew Bible. In the English Bible it is placed between Judges and Samuel. The period of Judges was a period of anarchy (political instability, religious apostasy, economic hardship and lawlessness) and the book of Samuel begins with the prayer and commitment of a godly woman Hannah. Ruth is better than the Covenant community in the book of Judges and is in line with the godly character Hannah. In the Hebrew Bible it is placed after Proverbs, where Ruth serves as a historical example of the woman of noble character portrayed in Proverbs 31.[227]

Ruth, the migrant turned emptiness to fullness. Her loyalty affirmed the appreciation from both Jewish men and women (chapter 4). The words of blessings are expressed in the form of prayer 'May the LORD make this woman, who is coming into your home, like Rachel and Leah, who had many children and built up the people of Israel......may the LORD give you many children through Ruth. May your family be great like this...may he (Obed) become famous in Israel......She (Ruth) is better to you than seven sons, because she has given birth to your grandson (Ruth 4:11-15).

Conclusion

In the book of Ruth, though three women's role can be seen but was dominated by two different religions and cultures. Naomi, a Jewish woman with the help of Ruth a Moabite changed not only her history but also Israel's history. Orpah and Ruth adopted two different paths. Orpah decided to stick to her religion and culture. Ruth unlike Orpah took a different stand by following Naomi and changed the negative picture of Moab. Moabites that were barred to be admitted to the assembly of the Lord (Deut 23:3) received the honor of lineage with the savior of the world. The challenge of Ruth against the so called patriarchal power made history anew. Ruth, a Moabite with the help of Naomi changed the curse to blessing. Ruth specially being a Moabite considered as a degenerated group turned up the picture of an individual who with Boaz brought forth the Messiah of the world. The decision and determination of Ruth, the margin changed the destiny of Naomi and her people.

---

[227] Santha Kumari Mondithoka, 'Ruth,' in *South Asia Bible Commentary*, Brian Wintle (ed.), Udaipur: Open Door Publications, 2015, 331.

Chapter 4

Esther and Mordecai: The Subalterns

Subaltern and Its Beginning

The term 'Subaltern'[228] was coined by the Italian political theorist (Marxist) Antonio Gramsci (1891-1937).[229] The term 'subaltern' generally means subordinate social groups. For R. Guha, the colonist, nationalist and Marxist historiography ignored the importance and contribution of the peasants and tribal in South Asia. He defines

[228] The word 'subalten' means 'as those who are below the altar,' i.e., people who could be altered. The people who are subordinated in terms of class, caste, gender etc. The subaltern is always in plural form denoting a group or groups of people who are oppressed. See K. Jesurathnam, "Dalit and Subaltern Hermeneutics in Conversation with Reader Response Method: I Kings 22, A Case in Point," *Bangalore Theological Forum* 1 (2016), 46-60.

[229] Gramsci began to weave ideas about subaltern identity into theories of class struggle. For further reading see David Ludden, "Introduction: A Brief History of Subaltenity," in *Reading Subaltern Studies: Critical History, Contested Meaning, and the Globalization of South Asia*, ed. David Ludded (Delhi: Permanent Black, 2003), 1-39.

subaltern as that of 'inferior rank.'[230] Spivak focuses primarily on the experiences of the subaltern women whose voices and social locations were ignored by both the colonial and the elite social groups. She points out that the active involvements of women against British colonialism were ignored to keep the male dominant.[231]

In the second half of the 20th century, there has been a powerful and unswerving resistance from the people of the voiceless group to redefine the elitist historiography which was written by the so called influential groups. Subsequently the writings became a people centered one.[232] This approach is the voice of the people who belongs to the subordinate social groups. It is a hermeneutics from below. It refers to a situation of inferior rank. It emerges from out of the lowly, inferiorly or marginally placed situation of any group in society.[233] They refute, reject or disown all the religious interpretation of the dominant groups and bring out the picture and words of forced marginalization and powerlessness. This approach re-reads and re-interprets the events which have been written from an elitistic perspective. Hence, this study is an effort to hear/listen to the people and their voices which were silenced by the colonial and dominant groups. It enables them to converse in their own language, the language of remonstration, resistance and repudiation. It has commonality with Postcolonial approach which will be discussed later.

The prominent people who advocated for subaltern readings are the Italian Marxist thinker Antonio Gramsci, Gayatri Charavorty Spivak and Ranajit Guha. Gramsci employed the term 'subaltern'

---

[230] See Ranajit Guha, "Preface," in *Subaltern Studies I: Writings on South Asian History and Society*, ed. Ranajit Guha (New Delhi, 1982), vii.

[231] For further readings refer Gayatri Chakravorty Spivak, "Postcolonial Theory and Literature," in *New Dictionary of the History of Ideas*, ed. Maryanne Cline Horowitz (London: Gale Cengage Learning, 2005), 1863.

[232] C. I. David Joy, "The Social and Religious Origins of the Gospel of Mark and Its Hermeneutical Implications: A Post-Colonial Critique," *Bangalore Theological Forum* 33, no. 1 (2001), 11-12.

[233] Felix Wilfred, "Towards a Subaltern Hermeneutics: Beyond the Contemporary Polarities in the Interpretation of Religious Tradition," *Jeeva Dhara* 26, no. 151 (1996), 46.

primarily for the oppressed rural peasant group in South Italy. The rural peasant groups were disposed to the ruling groups and their ideas and culture. He also used this term interchangeably with 'subordinate' and the 'non-hegemonic groups or classes.'[234] Both Guha and Spivak went beyond Gramsci's class ideology and opted for class, caste and gender. Both of them questioned and attacked the National Independence movement and the Western critical theory adopted by the Indian historians. Spivak raised a crucial question: Why Indian nationalism failed to represent the majority of India's population? Her argument is based on the contribution of the Subaltern groups to Mahatma Gandhi in the policy of resistance against the British colonial rule. It was the subaltern groups and not merely the small educated middle class who joined Gandhi to resist the British colonial rule. She advocated rewriting history from below, as the subaltern resistance to colonial rule and oppression are unrecorded in the records of official history.[235] Spivak also questioned the rationale behind the adoption of Western critical theory and Western Marxist model. For her, the Western Marxist model will not help to recover and address the complex histories of the Subaltern especially the resistance made by the Subalterns.[236] She also argued that 'the everyday lives of many Third world women are so complex and unsystematic that they cannot be known or represented by the vocabularies of western critical theory.'[237] She also went further to say that the lives and struggles of the 'Third World' women will be 'silenced and restricted within the technical vocabulary of the Western critical theory.'[238] She also questioned the classic Marxist approach which overlooked the lives and struggles of the third world women. Similarly Ranajit Guha, the Subaltern Studies historian questioned the national independence movement. For him, the small groups of educated middle-class men dominated

---

[234] Antonio Gramsci, *Selection from Prison Notebooks*, trans. Quintin Hoare and Geoffrey Nowell Smith (London: Lawrence and Wishart, 1978), xiv.

[235] Stephen Morton, *Gayatri Chakravorty Spivak* (London: Routledge, 2003), 6.

[236] Morton, *Gayatri Chakravorty Spivak*, 7.

[237] Morton, *Gayatri Chakravorty Spivak*.

[238] Morton, *Gayatri Chakravorty Spivak*.

and controlled the political and economic realm giving no benefit whatsoever to the rural peasant laborers.[239]

The Subaltern reading advocates writing history from below as they strongly feels that the histories of the rural peasantry, working class, and women were documented first by the British colonial powers and then rewritten by the elite social groups to meet their terms and interest.

Subaltern Reading of the Hebrew Bible

Esther: The Margin Exposing the Center

The meaning of Esther is star, secret and hidden. In similar line the book of Esther is a book of star, secret/hidden. The silent and hidden character Esther exposes the powerful, influential and outspoken character Haman.

The important and striking feature in the book of Esther is its *reversal strategy*. The status and characters undergo sudden changes. Vashti from queen to no one; Esther from an orphan to a queen; Haman though highest among the officials was asked to honor his enemy Mordecai; Haman prepared gallows to hang Mordecai but he was himself hanged on them; and the king was helpless to reverse the law concerning Vashti but he indirectly reversed the law against the Jews by passing an edict in favor of Jews permitting them to defend themselves.

Other than the feature of reversal, we could also locate at least five instances where things which were in secret and hidden exposed in due time.

1. Esther was asked by Mordecai to keep secret her identity (2:10) and in due time her identity was revealed (8:1).
2. The officers of the king made secret plans to kill king Xerxes but Mordecai exposed the plan. The twofold consequences were that the officers were hanged (2:23) and the good deeds of Mordecai were recorded (2:22-23) but honoured much later (6:11). A careful reader will be puzzled to know the reason why Haman was promoted in

---

[239] Morton, *Gayatri Chakravorty Spivak*, 6-7.

chapter 3 right after the incident where Mordecai saved the king? The promotion should be given to Mordecai not Haman! It is a 'delay tactic' to expose in full the mind-set of the colonizer. Mordecai, the colonized was honoured by Haman, the promoted colonizer in broad day light and in full public view!

3. Haman the colonizer plotted secretly to kill the Jews (chs 3 and 5) but Mordecai and Esther, representatives of the colonized group exposed the secret plot (ch 7).
4. Haman made a divisive and strategic plan to wipe out all the Jews and he fixed the day of lot (Pur), the thirteenth day of the twelfth month which was known as the month of Adar, to blot out the Jews (3:7, 13). Mordecai and Esther knew that the letter issued by Haman in the name of the king and sealed with his signet ring could not be altered. So, they pleaded with the king to pass another order permitting the Jews to defend themselves from the evil plan of Haman and the day fixed was the thirteenth day of the twelfth month, the month of Adar (8:7, 8, 12, and 13). The colonized mimiticized the divisive strategy of the colonizer by tactfully passing the edict and fixing the day of execution. The day planned to secretly kill the Jews was pur/im and it became the day to kill the enemies of the Jews.
5. The name of God and His acts are hidden throughout the book but in every chapter we can locate the unknown force who stood with the colonized group: a) Queen Vashti was dethroned and replaced by Queen Esther b) God gave a sleepless night to the king resulting in him seeing the daily court record (6:1) which in turned prepared the colonized Mordecai to help Esther realize that a Subaltern can speak and have a voice in the court of the ruler, and c) Esther the Silent one was given boldness by the unknown force to represent the colonized group resulting in her receiving a favour from the king.

Reading the Selected Passages of Esther from a Subaltern Perspective (1:1-2:23; 4:13-5:8; 7:1-8:8)

Esther 1:1-2:23: Refusal and Replacement

The unit Esther 1:1-2:23 introduces four important characters: Xerxes, Vashti, Mordecai and Esther. It consists of three scenes:[240]

Scene no. 1: This scene recounts the events that lead to the deposal of Queen Vashti, necessary for Esther's rise to the position of Queen.

Scene no. 2: It depicts the manner in which Esther replaces Vashti as the queen of Persia necessary for her role in foiling Haman's plot to destroy the Jews.

Scene no. 3: It presents the unrewarded service that Mordecai renders to the king, which service is indispensable to the events related in 6:1-13. This scene is symbolically significant for in it Mordecai is exalted and Haman executed.

In this unit, king Xerxes asked Queen Vashti to present herself before the nobles, officials and the people. Queen Vashti refused it. The Persian law permits Persian wives to attend banquets (Neh. 2:6) but would leave before the time of drinking. Only harem women and concubines are present when men drink (Dn 5:2). For a queen to appear at king's command was to be toyed with and treated as a mere harem woman or concubine. The king's insistence that she wear her royal crown heightens the degradation by calling attention to her true status.[241] Since she realized the command of the king was irrational, she refused. Her refusal to obey was justified. There are mixed opinions concerning her refusal. According to Josephus, she refused to come because the Persian law forbade wives to be seen by strangers. According to Rabbis, she was meant to wear only the royal crown and to expose her body.[242] The text however, is not clear.

---

[240] Fredrich Bush, "Esther," in *Word Biblical Commentary: Ruth and Esther*, ed. David A. Hubbard and Glen W. Barker, Vol. 9 (Dallas: Word Books, 1996), 342.

[241] Michael V. Fox, *Character and Ideology in the Book of Esther* (Grand Rapids, Michigan: William B. Eerdmans Publishing Company, 1991), 168-169.

[242] Sidnie White Crawford, "The Book of Esther," in *The New Interpreter's Bible,* ed. Leander E. Keck, Vol. 3 (Nashville: Abingdon Press, 1990), 882. As

Vashti is opposing the male power structure where female freedom and decision is dictated by the male counterparts.

The author of this book is not dwelling much in the incidences happened to Vashti rather interested to point out how Esther occupied the position of Queen. He wants to highlight that Esther the Queen with the advice of Mordecai saved the Jews from the hand of her enemy.

However, it will be worthwhile to know the act of Vashti. As mentioned, the Rabbis believed that Vashti was asked to expose her body. She told the king "If I come before the lords of the kingdom they will kill you and marry me." According to the Persian custom, the wedded wives could be present at dinners, but are not present when the drinking bout was to begin, as the concubines and courtesans are present. So, by coming to the king's party, Vashti would degrade herself to the position of a concubine. Being a woman of dignity she refused the command of king. But, her refusal questioned the legal issue. In the Persian view, the king is the law himself. Vashti by refusing the king's command have broken the law.[243] The king consulted the sages who know the laws (v. 13). The legal advisers told the king, if action will not be taken against her, all the women will disobey their husband. The motive behind this legal advice is to project male dominancy over female counterparts.

Queen Vashti was caught in a dilemma; to obey would mean losing her identity and dignity which could even harm the life and dignity of king or to disobey the king's command which would ultimately result to her removal from the position of Queen. Queen Vashti considered her identity as more important than her position.

---

mentioned the MT gives no reason for Vashti's refusal. The Megilla, I and II Targums, and other ancient commentaries states that Vashti was commanded to wear only the royal crown, and was, commanded to appear stark naked. Josephus in *Antiquities* XI.191 says that strangers were not allowed to look at the beauty of Persian wives. [Refer Carey A. Moore, *The Anchor Bible: Esther* (New York: Double day & Company, 1971), 13]. According to one view in Talmud because she had taken Israelite maidens and stripped them naked she was punished by herself being summoned naked. She is identified as the grand daughter of Nebuchadnezzar. [refer Michael V. Fox, *Character and Ideology*, 164-165].

[243] Elias Bickerman, *Four Strange Books of the Bible* (New York: Schocken Books, 1967), 185-186.

She lost her position to maintain her identity. In chapter 2:1, the text says that the king remembered Vashti and what she had done and that what had been decreed against her. It probably points out that the king felt sorry for the act done against her.

The sacrifice of Vashti prepared the way for Esther. Esther the margin won the favor of the powerful king through her beauty and gradually changed the male dominated and imperialistic mindset of divide and rule policy.

Esther 3-5: Act of Haman and Confidence of Esther

Chapters 3-5 is the central section of the book with the fate of the Jews sealed in the edict of Haman.

Chapter 4 consists of three scenes: Scene 1 (4:1-3); scene 2 (4:4-9); and scene 3 (4:10-17).

The first scene (vv. 1-3) is a separate scene from what follows primarily by its context (chapter 3), which relates the anguish and the shock with which Mordecai and all other Jews reacted to Haman's decree.

The second scene (vv. 4-9) is primarily a dialogue between Esther and Mordecai.

The scene third (vv. 10-17) consists of a three-part communication between Esther and Mordecai (v. 11, 13-14 and 16). Unlike the first two scenes, the third scene is a direct course. The whole sections are summed up with a narrative summary in v. 17.[244]

In these verses Mordecai warned Esther that she could not hide herself. According to Herodotus, in the tradition of Medes, unannounced entry before the king was unlawful, but a petitioner might send in a message and request an audience.[245] Though according to the Persian Law, she faced danger if she approached the king uninvited, but she also was in danger if she keeps silent. Mordecai made his point, and Esther is placed in a difficult situation. The Persian law is irreversible and it could cost her life to disobey but keeping silent could cost the life of the whole Jewish race. Esther with strong determination opted for the second option and that is

---

[244] Fredrich Bush, "Esther," 393.

[245] Sidnie White Crawford, "The Book of Esther," 904.

clearly seen in her statement in verse 16- 'if I perish, I perish'. Esther could have opted for the first option but her decision shows courage and faith in a male dominated colonial structure.

Vashti is banished for refusing to appear before the king when summoned, and now Esther is asked by Mordecai to risk her life by appearing before the king uninvited. The text also states that she has not been summoned for 30 days which perhaps indicate her weakening influence. In spite of all these reasons, she took the courage and stood before the king. Perhaps Mordecai was pressurizing Esther to act using rhetoric method? There is a possibility. Mordecai considers Esther's position as a means provided by God for Jewish deliverance. The history throughout conveys the message that God acts through human agent. Hence, Mordecai is not postulating that deliverance will arise for the Jews from some unexpressed source, rather affirms that Esther is the only possible source of deliverance for the Jews. He is attempting to motivate her to act.[246] She was challenged to confront the king courageously. Mordecai's words to Esther- '*Who knows perhaps you have come to royal dignity for just such a time as this,'* is in the form of a rhetorical question. Her initiative is the only hope the Jews[247] If we read carefully, Mordecai in the first part of this verse signals that if you keep silent, relief and deliverance will arise from another place and then uses a rhetorical form-'who knows?' This rhetorical question doesn't express doubt about the providential purpose of her position as queen rather it expresses a confident hope. The expression '*You have come to a royal position*' indicates the theme of election. In the biblical perspective election is for service, not just for one's own benefit. Being an agent of liberation for her people was more important than being the queen of Persia.[248]

The response of Esther '*I will go to the king*' marks her strong determination. She risked her life with male dominated leadership

---

[246] Fredrich Bush, "Esther," 397.

[247] Fredrich Bush, "Esther."

[248] Mervin Breneman, "Esther," in *An Exegetical and theoretical exposition of the Holy Scripture: Ezra, Nehemiah and Esther*, ed. L. Ray Clandenen, Vol.10 (USA: Broadman Holman Publishers, 1993), 337.

and strict Persian law for the deliverance of her people. The words, '*and if I perish, I perish* is neither a hopeless expression to the inevitable challenge ahead nor seeking an escape route rather a courageous determination to face danger. Here Esther identifies with her people. She considered her people's safety more important than her well-being.

If we read carefully, three people considered as marginalia took up the challenge. Vashti displayed courage in her refusal to humiliate herself by disobeying the order of the king, Mordecai displayed his courage in a life threatening situation by not bowing down to Haman thereby sticking to and affirming the monotheistic faith, and in this verse Esther proved bravery by risking her life to save her people.

On the third day Esther put on her royal robes and stood in the inner court of the king's palace, opposite the king's hall. The king was sitting on his royal throne inside the palace opposite the entrance to the palace (ch 5). The words 'and stood' must not be overlooked. This expression shows her act of bravery by breaking the Persian law and standing in the king's court without being invited.[249] She appeared before the king illegally and moreover she was in fast, which could in fact harm her beauty but like Daniel (Dn.1:7-8) she resolved to appear before the king for she knew and recognized a higher responsibility, i.e., her responsibility towards her people and her obligation towards her God.

The king said to her, "What is it, Queen Esther? What is your request? It shall be given you, even to the half of my kingdom". "What is it, Queen Esther? Literally it means what to you? The king sensed that Esther's appearance before him without being called must have been for a serious reason. Then Esther said, "If it pleases the king, let the king and Haman come today to a banquet that I have prepared for the king". Esther did not wish to make her request there in the court. Instead she requested the king to attend a banquet and also invited Haman. The king is not aware of the reason behind the banquet which clearly shows the intelligence of Esther. The king was willing to grant half of the kingdom but for Esther the head of Haman was more important than 'half' of the kingdom.

---

[249] Mervin Breneman, "Esther," 339.

While they were drinking wine, the king said to Esther, "What is your petition? It shall be granted you. And what is your request? Even to the half of my kingdom, it shall be fulfilled." Then Esther said, "This is my petition and request: If I have won the king's favor, and if it pleases the king to grant my petition and fulfill my request, let the king and Haman come tomorrow to the banquet that I will prepare for them and then I will do as the king has said." Why did Esther make the king wait? In plain reading, the delaying was a risk, for the kings' mood could have changed. For Esther the time was not ripe enough. Her second petition leads to another banquet stated in chapter 7. Why was Haman invited and why was he silent throughout? Haman's silence is mysterious. The rabbis give various reasons for his attendance. Esther was acting in accordance with Proverbs 25:21, 'If your enemies are hungry, give them bread to eat; and if they are thirsty, give them water to drink.' She was still keeping her Jewishness secret, she may have wished to make the king jealous, or maybe she was setting a trap for Haman. Modern commentators too have tried to discern Esther's motive that she wanted to lure Haman into a false sense of security.[250] Esther tactfully played a wise role and the entire episode is part of a clever stratagem.

7:1-8:8: Haman Hanged and Jews Succeeded

So, the king and Haman went in to feast with Queen Esther. On the second day, as they were drinking wine, the king again said to Esther, "What is your petition, Queen Esther? It shall be granted you. And what is your request? Even to the half of my kingdom, it shall be fulfilled." Like the earlier occasion, the king once again repeats his offer. Here Esther instead of delaying or postponing made up her mind to narrate the reason for the banquet. Then Queen Esther answered, "If I have won your favor, O king, and if it pleases the king, let my life be given me-that is my petition-and the lives of my people-that is my request." The response of Esther startled and perplexed the king. Unlike the earlier response, Queen Esther puts one phrase, "in your eyes", in the second person, which shows

---

[250] Sidnie White Crawford, "The Book of Esther", 909.

of greater intimacy.[251] Esther asks for her life and for her people. Esther uses the two terms used by king- 'petition' and 'request'. She connects the first term with herself and the second term with her people. Both the terms are equivalent to each other, which intimates that her people's lives are as precious to her as her own life. She is demonstrating creative word play-intimacy between the king-herself-her people. She intimates to the king that to kill her people is to kill her.[252] In a sense she equates herself with her people. Here, once again, Esther used her wisdom in communicating the reason behind the banquet. Mordecai strongly advised her not to reveal her identity but Esther in spite of knowing that it was life and death matter, risked her life, which clearly demonstrates her heroic action.

For we have been sold, I and my people, to be destroyed, to be killed, and to be annihilated. If we had been sold merely as slaves, men and women, I would have held my peace; but no enemy can compensate for this damage to the king. Esther using her wisdom identified herself with her people not by their name, the Jews, but rather by their fate, for she knows that the king has passed the edict against the Jews. Gradually she revealed her relation with Mordecai. *For we have been sold* is a phrase sometimes used for being handed over or betrayed. Here Esther was also making allusions to the money Haman offered to the king.[253]

Then king Xerxes said to Queen Esther, "Who is he, and where is he, who has presumed to do this?" The literal translation of verse 5 is 'then king Xerxes spoke and he said to Esther the queen..." Some think that the repetition of the verb "spoke" or "he said" is a dittography, but it can be the purpose of the narrator to intensify the suspense.[254] Here the title and name of the person is mentioned

---

[251] Michael V. Fox, *Character and Ideology*, 83.

[252] Michael V. Fox, *Character and Ideology*.

[253] Mervin Breneman, "Esther," 348.

[254] Mervin Breneman, "Esther." Ehrlich and Ringgren read *wayyemaher*, "and he hurried" in place of the first *wayyomer*. Bardtke retained both verbs and translated them as "then spoke king Ahasuerus; and he said to Queen Esther" (refer Carey A. Moore, *The Anchor Bible: Esther*, 71).

which reminds us that this is a dialogue of 'Majesties' giving less importance to Haman.[255]

Esther said, "A foe and enemy, this wicked Haman!" Then Haman was terrified before the king and the queen. The question "who is he, and where is he, who has presumed to do this?" placed her in a dangerous position. She did not know how the king would react, for Haman was highly regarded and had more influence. Unlike earlier passages the answer of Esther was direct, short and clear. Here she revealed her identity which had not revealed at the behest of Mordecai.

The king rose from the feast in wrath and went into the palace garden, but Haman stayed to beg his life from Queen Esther, for he saw that the king had determined to destroy him. Why was the king so angry? He was angry because he had been tricked into making the decree that meant the death of his own beloved.[256] Why had Esther delayed in communicating Haman's trick? Esther sensed that Haman is highly acknowledged, so she decided first to win the heart of king. At the appropriate time, she revealed her heart, which showed her wisdom in the male dominated culture and government of that time.

When the king returned from the palace garden to the banquet hall, Haman had thrown himself on the couch where Esther was reclining; and the king said, "Will he even assault the queen in my presence, in my own house? As the words left the mouth of the king, they covered Haman's face. Then Harbona, one of the eunuchs in attendance on the king, said, "Look, the very gallows that Haman has prepared for Mordecai, whose word saved the king, stands at Haman's house, fifty cubits high." And the king said, "Hang him on that." So they hanged Haman on the gallows that he had prepared for Mordecai. Then the anger of the king abated. Haman in typical West Asian form, probably grabbed the feet of Esther, kissed and begged for forgiveness. Such action would explain why the king interprets Haman as about to assault/molest Esther. Haman who expected Mordecai to bow before him is now at the feet of a Jewish woman

---

[255] Michael V. Fox, *Character and Ideology*, 85.

[256] Mervin Breneman, "Esther," 349.

Esther.[257] The proud Haman, who was irritated with Mordecai's refusal to bow, now falls at the feet of a Jewish woman pleading for his life.

In chapter 1 Xerxes had his dignity affronted by the denial of Vashti, when to protect her dignity, she refused his command. In this chapter, the king saw his queen assaulted (7:8). Here the king realized that his dignity lies with the dignity of queen. Haman is led to execution. In the first case, queen Vashti was removed from her position by the advice of seven counselors. In the latter case, the king, without taking any advice ordered the execution. With Haman being executed, Esther then requested that the Jews be spared the consequences of the edict planned by Haman. Since the king is unable to reverse the edict, he passed another edict authorizing the Jews to defend themselves against anyone who attacks them.

Then Esther spoke again to the king; she fell at his feet, weeping and pleading with him to avert the evil design of Haman the Agagite and the plot that he had devised against the Jews. This statement is interpreted in two different ways. Some suggest this verse as a new scene and others consider it as a continuation of the scene described in verses 1-2. Esther implores the king on behalf of her people. She pleads with him to avert the evil design of Haman and the plot that he had devised against the Jews. Though she uses the two terms evil and plot separately but the idea which she communicates to the king is the evil plot.

The king held out the golden scepter to Esther, and Esther rose and stood before the king. She said, "If it pleases the king, and if I have won his favor, and if the thing seems right before the king, and If I am pleasing to him, let an order be written to revoke the letters devised by Haman son of Hammedatha the Agagite, which he wrote giving orders to destroy the Jews who are in all the provinces of the king." The king indicates his favor towards her by stretching out the golden scepter. If we compare verse 5 with chapter 5:4, 5:8, 7:3, differences can be seen. In 5:4, the phrase used by Esther is "If

---

[257] Mervin Breneman, "Esther," 350. Many scholars argue that Haman, in a typical Near Eastern gesture of humility and contrition, either seized Esther's feet or even kissed them. Probably King sat this act and stated the improper advances of Haman (refer Carey A. Moore, *The Anchor Bible: Esther,* 72).

it pleases the king…", in 5:8 "If I have won the king's favor, and if it pleases the king…", in 7:3, "If I have won your favor, O King, and if it pleases the king…", but in 8:5, four phrases are used "If it pleases the king and If I have found favor with him, and if the idea seem proper to the king, and if I am pleasing to him…" which shows her intimacy towards the king and her confidence and hope for her people. Esther was extremely tactful for she did not use the word 'law' for she knows that the Persian law could not be repealed and it was King who signed the edict. She put all the blame on Haman.

Then king Ahasuerus (Xerxes) said to Queen Esther and to the Jew Mordecai, "See, I have given Esther the house of Haman, and they have hanged him on the gallows, because he plotted to lay hand on the Jews." Here the king uses the title Queen for Esther as usual but for Mordecai the title used is 'Jew'. It clearly shows the acceptance of the Jews in the eyes of the king.

You may write as you please with regard to the Jews, in the name of the king, and seal it with the king's ring; for an edict written in the name of the king and sealed with the king's ring cannot be revoked. The king addresses him in a plural form "you". The plural 'you' before the imperative is very emphatic suggesting that you can do what is pleasing with regard to the Jews.

Esther was very wise in handling the case. Mordecai cautioned her but Esther tactfully prepared the strategy, which shows how the *marginalia*/voiceless group can be a powerful voice in a male dominated and colonized structure. The whole situation is reversed by two individuals Esther and Mordecai.

Revisiting the Characters: Center and the Margin

Vashti and Esther

Vashti stays out when invited, Esther enters when uninvited. Vashti risked only the wrath of the king; Esther risks the king's sentence of death.[258] Vashti displaced and Esther replaced. Vashti maintained her identity but couldn't alter the law (1:19). Esther through her boldness could not reverse the Persian law (8:8), but was able to have another edict passed to defend against Haman's edict. Esther

[258] David J. A. Clines, *The Esther Scroll* (Sheffield: JSOT Press, 1984), 35.

probably sensed the danger of going against the law, but finally with the advice of Mordecai, she took courage and the king passed the law to defend the Jewish community. She nullifies the universally dreaded law (4:11) by entering the king's presence. Her bold step was an eye opener for the male dominated law system. Her heroic and skillful tactics were significant for the lives of the Jewish community. Vashti refused to be a sexual object for men and Esther, though a woman in man's world, succeeded in changing the male dominated approach towards the marginalized group. Vashti's courage must be highly acknowledged. She is a woman of dignity. She refused the command of her husband, the king, to shame herself in publicly. She was willing to give up her status in order to do what was right. She regarded her dignity as more important than her place and position in society. Her act of courage in refusing to present her before the king is equaled to Esther's boldness to appear before the king without permission. Both made a stand that more than power, it is determination, justice and human dignity, which counts. They exhibited the power of rightness.[259]

Esther and Mordecai

Mainstream scholars attribute the victory of the Jews to Mordecai. Though I am not negating this view, the role of Esther is highly commended. Without Esther there would be no story. At the moment of crisis, Mordecai can only go to Esther and ask her to intercede with the king. Esther then devises a plan and carries it out with boldness and admirable skill and in the end not only saved the Jews but also arrange for Mordecai to inherit Haman's position. If we observe carefully, Mordecai instructs Esther to go to the king to make supplication to him and entreat him for her people (4:8). Esther does not follow Mordecai's instruction precisely. Her motives were a wise approach. She does not grasp at the king's offer to be given even half of the kingdom. If she wanted, she could have seized the opportunity but instead, she made a calculated plan to win the heart of the king and to trap the enemy Haman. Why was Haman invited to the banquet? Her deliberate invitation of Haman clearly

---

[259] Mervin Breneman, "Esther," 308.

reveals her wisdom. Had she invited the king alone, there was a possibility the king would share the matter with Haman, and as usual he would have taken the advice of counselors, which could have invited further danger for her and her people. She arranged it in such a way that Haman was trapped and king became helpless. The initiative of Mordecai and the boldness of Esther changed the picture of gloom to a position of joy. It illustrates how marginal people can change history, a history which is controlled and manipulated by powerful and hierarchical male dominated societies.

Esther, Haman and the King

Haman had the king pass an edict to kill the Jews and prepared gallows to put an end to Mordecai. Esther in order to foil the plan of Haman prepared a reversal strategy. The strategy was a banquet strategy. It was a well-designed and a calculated move which points out her courageous spirit, consummate skill and commendable shrewdness. The strategy of two banquet is not a doublet and triplet as found in Genesis (two names of God, famine etc.), rather a well-planned trick. The first banquet was to make Haman proud (5:9-14) ending up in honoring Mordecai (6:9-14). The second banquet was to put an end to Haman, the Colonizer (ch 7) and the reversal of the edict (chs 8-9). In chapters 5-8, we could locate number of reversals: 'gallows for Mordecai became the gallows for Haman, (5:14; 7:9-10)' 'the counsel of Zeresh, wife of Haman (5:14; 6:13),' 'signet ring (8:2),' and 'edict and date of edict (chs 8).' All these reversals took place by the skill and shrewd tactics of Esther. Herbert Lockyer commends Esther by saying 'Esther is a woman of clear judgment, of magnificent self-control and capable of the noblest self-sacrifice.'[260]

Subaltern Strategy

Plot and Dramatic Reversal of Esther and Mordecai

The book of Esther is dominated by three characters namely Haman, Mordecai and Esther. There are three main plots: plot of Haman;

---

[260] Herbert Lockyer, *All the Women of the Bible* (Secunderabad: OM Books, 1967), 52.

plot of Mordecai and plot of Esther. Haman[261] was an influential person in the Persian court. His advice was given due importance by the Persian king and knowing his influence, people bowed before him. Moreover, it is a normal practice to make obeisance before high-ranking officials. If so, why did Mordecai refuse to bow? There are two possible reasons: Mordecai a staunch monotheistic worshipper and follower of Mosaic Law decided not to revere the mortal Haman; secondly, he was an Agagite and therefore, an enemy.[262] The refusal to bow resulted for a major genocide plot. In order to accomplish the plot, Haman gave ten thousand talents[263] to help the king and to secure the king's consent to pass the edict. He also fixed the date for execution.

The dramatic reversal of the plot took place because of two individuals: one individual outside the Palace and one individual inside the palace, like Pharaoh's daughter and Moses in Exodus. Though Mordecai is the instigator of the reversal, Esther is the important factor in the effecting of the reversal of the plot and the edict.[264]

---

[261] Haman is mentioned as Agagite perhaps referring to Amalekite who is bitter enemies of Israel (c.f. Dt. 25:17-19) refer John Bendor-Samuel, "Esther," in *New International Bible Commentary*, ed. F. F. Bruce (Grand Rapids, Michigan: Zondervan, 1979), 514.

[262] John Bendor-Samuel, "Esther," 515; David Clarence, "Exodus," in *South Asia Bible Commentary*, ed. Brian Wintle (Udaipur: Open Door Publication, 2015), 571. Mordecai is identified as a Benjamite from the clan of Kish (2:5), the father of Saul; Haman is a descendant of Agag (3:1), the Amalekite king against whom Saul had fought (I Sm 15). The history of conflict between Israel and the Amalekite is seen from the time of Exodus. Moses said 'The Lord will be at war with the Amalekites from generation to generation (Ex 17:16).' Israel was charged with 'blotting out the memory of the Amalek from under heaven' (Dt. 25:17-19; I Sm 15:23). There are scores of references throughout the Bible indicating the conflicts (Jgs 3:13; 5:14; I Sm 27:8; 30:13-18). The conflict between Haman, the Agag and Mordecai, a descendant of Benjamite can be read against this background. For further reading refer Raymond B. Dillard and Tremper Longman III, *An Introduction to the Old Testament* (Grand Rapids, Michigan: Zondervan, 1994), 196-197.

[263] Ten thousand talents would have been equivalent to the total tribute paid by the whole Persian Empire indirectly referring to the killing of the whole Jews (refer David Clarence, "Exodus," 572.

[264] Frederich Bush, "Esther," 318-319.

Esther: Dramatic Change from Passive to Active

The narrator beautifully pictures the role of Esther. Esther though appointed as queen in place of Vashti was not given an independent character but is portrayed as Mordecai's character. The passive role can be seen right from the selection to the appointment as queen. The narrator used three passive verbs in verse 8 'So when the king's order and his edict *were proclaimed*, and when many young women *were gathered* in the citadel of Susa in the custody of Hegai, Esther *was also taken* into the king's palace and put in custody of Hegai, who had charge of the women.' The narrator's choice of words paints her coming to the palace as an 'ineluctable fate.'[265] The narrator change her passive character 'as custody of Hegai' to her active position 'She *pleased* him (the king) and *won his favor* and he quickly provided her with her cosmetic treatments…and *advanced her* and her maids to *the best place* in the harem (2:9).' Of course Esther took the advice of Hegai (2:15) which is a wise and cooperative stand.[266] Her wise cooperative stand of silence elevated her position.

The dramatic change of 'passive-active' is also seen in relationship with Mordecai. The narrator presents the character Esther in the shadow of Mordecai 'Now *there was a Jew* in the citadel of Susa whose name was Mordecai son of Jair son of Shimei son of Kish a Benjamite. Kish had been carried away from Jerusalem among the captives carried away with king Jeconiah of Judah, whom king Nebuchadnezzar of Babylon had carried away. Mordecai had *brought up Hadassah that is Esther*, his cousin, for *she had neither father nor mother*; the girl was fair and beautiful, and when her father and her mother died, Mordecai *adopted her* as his own daughter (2:5-7).' The narrator instead of highlighting Esther and her family narrated in detail the three generations of Mordecai and the reason for being in the citadel of Susa. Thereafter, the narrator beautifully pointed out words like 'brought up (parenting),' 'change of name from Hadassah to Esther (authority over her),' 'had neither father nor mother (status as orphan),'and 'adopted,' which refers the status of Esther as more of 'Object (Passive).' The character of being an object is intensely

---

[265] Frederich Bush, "Esther," 319.

[266] John Bendor-Samuel, "Esther," 514.

changed in the course of dialogue between Mordecai and Esther. The subservient Esther became a queen maker as the conversation progresses, i.e., role of being a 'shadow' is turned to 'lime light' figure. The transforming aspect can be seen in the response of Esther to Mordecai's helpless stage (4:1-4). The response of submissive Esther turned into firm conviction, courageous determination and strong command.

When Mordecai tore his clothes and put on sackcloth and ashes, and went through the city, wailing with a loud and bitter cry, Esther was deeply distressed and sent garments *to clothe* Mordecai but Mordecai refused them (4:1-4). When Mordecai gave the reason, Esther responded with the rule of Persian court 'entering the inner court of king without permission is death unless the king holds out the golden scepter to someone (4:11).' But, when Mordecai posed a question pointing to the silence of Esther 'For if you keep silence at such a time as this...'Esther demonstrated the words of conviction, courage and command 'Go, gather all the Jews to be found in Susa (command), and hold a fast on my behalf, and neither eat nor drink for three days, night or day.[267] I and my maids will also fast as you do (conviction). After that I will go to the king, though it is against the law; and if I perish, I perish (determination) [4:15-16].' The narrator dramatically reverses the scene. The commanding character Mordecai ('*Charge* her to go to the king to make supplication to him and entreat him for her people [4:8] is reversed in 4:17 'Mordecai then went away and did everything as Esther had *ordered him*.'[268] Thereafter Esther continued the active role. This we could see in her appeal to the king (chapters 5 and 7) leading to the deliverance of the Jews.

Conclusion

If we observe carefully the book of Esther, we can see two different religions and cultures. Vashti, a gentile stood for her dignity and didn't compromise with the male voice of dominancy and inhumanity.

---

[267] 'Night or day' means strict fast observed through the night as well as day (John Bendor-Samuel, "Esther," 516).

[268] Frederich Bush, "Esther," 320.

Though she lost her place, she stood vindicated. Esther, a Jewish woman who received the throne at the expense of Vashti echoed her voice and authority thereby curtailing the male and imperial dominated structure. Though Mordecai warned her not to reveal her identity, she was bold enough to reveal who she was and presented her request. Her bold step and voice in a strange male and imperial dominated culture changed the fortune of her people. She attained her success without the element of divine miracle which is often seen in other narratives for instance, Daniel and Joseph's narrative.

The emerging picture is, if two marginalized people unite, though they are weaker together they can change the colonized dominated structure. Vashti lost the position of queen due to male dominated self-centered system. However, Esther an Orphan received the position of Queen and was not complacent rather raised her voice in a male dominated structure. Mordecai a Benjamite, considered as a lesser tribe, with the help of Esther changed the fortune of Jewish race, which is an eye opener for dominant tribes and colonized structure.

We are living in a world where the powerful dominates the powerless and rich dominates the poor. The marginalized group has a voice but they are not allowed to speak. The legal machinery and the media are hijacked by the rich and the powerful to suppress the rights of the subalterns. The right to equality and self-determination is at stake. In such an alarming situation, how do we face it? The tactic of Esther is the viable alternative. Esther the object became the subject. Her role changed from passive to active. She became the force to reverse the existing and dominating orders. When the male dominated group was able to silence and remove Vashti, Esther was able to speak and act resulting to the removal of Haman. Within the covenant community, Mordecai took the initiative and instigate Esther to act by using carefully coined wordings 'If you keep silence.' Hearing this, Esther came out of shadow to a dominant role influencing the Persian king to remove Haman the Colonizer and having her people freed from possible genocide.

In the history of Israel, two narratives project the deliverance of His people from their enemies: the Exodus narrative and Esther narrative. In the book of Exodus, Moses the adopted one, hid his identity and later revealed his identity by delivering his people from the hand of Egypt. In book of Esther, the adopted Esther hid her identity and later revealed her identity by delivering her people from possible genocide. If Moses' heroic act led to the beginning of Israelite history as nation, the heroic acts of Esther ended up with a happy note for the postexilic Covenant community. In the book of Exodus, after the Red Sea experience, the Decalogue clearly points out the importance of keeping the monotheistic belief (Exod 20). In the book of Esther, Mordecai and Esther realizing the importance of Decalogue decided to stand for the monotheistic belief leading to victory. In the book of Exodus, the act of Miriam and Moses with the help of God resulted to the feast of Passover. In the book of Esther, the act of Esther and Mordecai with the help of God resulted to the feast of Purim.

In short, God in His Sovereign grace uses both men and women to play instrumental role in delivering His people from the hand of their enemies. Both men and women are in the elective purpose of God provided they affirm their faith towards the triune God, the creator, provider and sustainer and stand firm in the word of God.

Chapter 5

Women's World: Center and Margin

Introduction

In women's world, we could locate center and margin. On one hand, the women movement fights for gender equality, but on the other hand, we could see differences within women. This aspect of differences can be seen even in the Hebrew Bible. In this chapter, the author wishes to focus on two books: Genesis (Book of Beginning) and Samuel (Book of Transition). In the book of Genesis, it was Sarah who asked Abraham to build a family through her. And later, Sarah pressurized Abraham to get rid of Hagar and her child. In the book of Samuel, Peninnah mocked Hannah for not having a child. Hannah instead of chasing out Peninnah like Hagar[269] decided to pour out her pain before God the Almighty. In each case, women are

[269] The other reading can be about free woman and slave woman. In the case of Sarah-Hagar episode, Hagar was a slave and without arguing left the house whereas in the episode of Hannah and Peninnah, both were free women. The only difference in this case is first and second wife.

the principal actors[270] and they are the ones who fought with each other. Their husbands merely agree to their counterpart.

Sarah and Hagar: Center and Margin

The episode of Sarah and Hagar[271] can be seen in chapters 16 and 21. It is not a doublet[272] rather two parts of a story separated apart. The first part is between Sarah and Hagar and the second part is extended further to the children of free (Sarah) and slave (Hagar) women. In both cases, we could see the helplessness of Abraham and the appearance of the angel of the Lord/God to Hagar. The appearance of God did not take place in the house of Abraham but in the wilderness. In the first part of the story, the angel of the Lord ask Hagar to return back and submit to her mistress which is attached with a promise and naming of the place. In the second part, God is not asking her to return rather assures her that He will bless her descendants. God was with the child in the wilderness. In both part of the story God assures Hagar that the promises which He made to Abraham will take place in her life too, i.e., promise of descendants and great nation.

[270] Gordon J. Wenham, "Genesis 16-150," in *Word Biblical Commentary*, ed. David A. Hubbard and Glenn W. Barker, Vol. 2 (Texas: Word Books, 1994), 4.

[271] The Scripture is silent about Hagar's genealogy. The legend mentions her as daughter of Pharaoh, the king of Egypt. It affirms that the Egyptian princess became so attached to Sarah that she told her royal father that she would accompany her when she returned to Abraham. When the king told her that she will be treated as a handmaid, she responded by saying that 'Better to be handmaid in the tents of Abraham than a princess in this palace.' Though this legend looks a pleasing one, but it is generally accepted that Hagar was an Egyptian slave whom Sarah secured for her while she and Abraham was in Egypt [Herbert Lockyer, *All the Women of the Bible* (Secunderabad: OM Books, 1967), 61].

[272] Gerhard von Rad and many others argue for two sources (Genesis 16 as J source and Genesis 21:8ff as E source). For more details read Gerhard von Rad, *Genesis: A Commentary* (Philadelphia: The Westminster Press, 1972).

Sarah: Center or Margin

Sarah though well aware of God's promise of descendants decided to take matters into her hands by proposing an alternative plan.[273] She asked Abraham to have a child through her slave. By doing this she ignored the promise of God and directed Abraham to have a child through Hagar. Sarah who simply obeyed Abraham and gone to Pharaoh in Genesis 12 is instructing Abraham and Abraham simply obeyed Sarah.[274] The scripture is not stating whether consent of Hagar was taken. As per the norm of the day, the slave was treated as property and hence the concern was not needed. Hagar is expected to fit in the plan of Sarah.[275] The question of refusal doesn't arise.

When Hagar became pregnant, Sarah realized her flaw in her plans. She also sensed that Hagar's attitude is changing (16:4b). Realizing her loss of status and gain of Hagar, Sarah blamed Abraham for all happenings. Hagar flees for her life and ended up in wilderness.[276] The Angel of the Lord appeared to Hagar in the wilderness and asked her to return and submit to her mistress Sarah.[277] Hagar obeyed the voice of God.

Then comes the second part of the story! When Isaac was weaned, Abraham arranged a great feast as a thanksgiving fellowship. Sarah noticed that Hagar's son Ishmael is playing with Isaac.[278] Sarah became angry. She decided not to share the inheritance of Isaac to Ishmael and insisted Abram to send both Hagar and her son away. Once again Abram became helpless and decided to heed the words of Sarah. Abraham sends away both of them with provisions which will last for a limited period of time. Once again, God appeared to Hagar.

---

[273] Allen P. Ross, "Genesis," in Bible Knowledge Commentary, ed. John F. Walvoord and Roy B. Zuck (Hyderabad: Authentic Books, 2012), 56.

[274] Jesudason Baskar Jeyaraj, "Genesis," in *South Asia Bible Commentary*, ed. Brian Wintle (Udaipur: Open Door Publications, 2015), 32.

[275] Jesudason Baskar Jeyaraj, "Genesis."

[276] Jesudason Baskar Jeyaraj, "Genesis."

[277] Yahweh in line with the legal regulation of the day asked Hagar to surrender before her mistress Sarah (Gerhard von Rad, *Genesis: A Commentary*, 194).

[278] The verb *ṣāḥaq* means playing or behaving wantonly with someone (Gerhard von Rad, *Genesis: A Commentary*, 232).

In the first part of the story, the accusation of Sarah was Hagar and in the second part of the story, it was towards Ishmael. The pertinent question is: What is the role of Sarah in both parts of the story. Sarah is playing the role of center by accusing Abraham for all this happenings and dominates the scene. Her voice prevailed in both parts of the story.

Hagar: Center or Margin

As mentioned earlier, Sarah instead of waiting upon God's plan decided to have her own plan. She asked Abraham to have one of her slaves as his concubine which Abraham approved.[279] The chosen concubine was Hagar possibly taken as slave during their stay in Egypt (Genesis 16:1-2). The idea of having child through concubine was a common practice in Ancient West Asia.[280] The child through a concubine will be regarded as child of mistress.[281] This point out clearly that slave is considered as property (c.f. Exodus 21:2-11; Genesis 30:3-12). The planning of Sarah and approval of Abraham doesn't carry the consent of Hagar the slave.

In this entire story, the role of Hagar is a subservient one. Her consent is not required as she is a slave and hence, property of her mistress. Hagar when realized that she is bearing a child became happy knowing the fact that she could bear child for her master which in turn led her to look with contempt on her mistress. Here we could see the conflict between the two women.[282] Sarah expressed

---

[279] Abraham like Adam (Genesis 3:17) obeyed the voice of Sarah ending up in separation from his son Ishmael in Genesis 21.

[280] The Sumero-Babylonian law Hammurabi code says 'If she has given a maid to her husband and she has borne children and afterwards that maid has made herself equal with her mistress, because she has borne children her mistress shall not sell her for money, she shall reduce her to bondage and count her among the female slaves.' Legally, if mistress gave her personal maid to her husband, in the event of her own childlessness, then the child born of the maid was considered the child of mistress. Refer Herbert Lockyer, *All the Women of the Bible,* 62), Henry Wansbrough, *Genesis: Doubleday Bible Commentary* (New York: Doubleday, 1998), 32; Gerhard von Rad, *Genesis: A Commentary*, 191.

[281] Allen P. Ross, "Genesis," 56.

[282] Allen P. Ross, "Genesis."

her pain to Abraham.[283] Abraham who failed to wait for God's plan once again failed to resolve the conflict. The mediation part which Abraham did to people of Sodom and Gomorrah is missing in this story. Abraham said to Sarah, 'Behold your maid is in your power, do to her as you please.' The language employed is a language of power and domination. Sarah dealt harshly/mistreated[284] with Hagar and she fled from her. Hagar who lost her identity by reducing as a slave is now in wilderness.

The Angel of the Lord appeared to Hagar in the wilderness. Sarah and Abraham addressed Hagar as maid (Genesis 16:2, 5 and 6) but the angel of the Lord addressed her by name (Genesis 16:8). The angel of the Lord said to Hagar to return and submit to her mistress and also gave a promise similar to the promise given to Abraham (Gen 16:10 c.f. Gen. 12 and 15).[285] In addition to the instruction and promise, the angel of the Lord who called her by name also gave the name of her son Ishmael means 'God hears,'[286] and also said clearly about the future of the child (Gen. 16:11-12). Like Abraham, Hagar called the name of the Lord who spoke to her and even named the place[287] where the angel of the Lord appeared to her (Gen. 16:13-14 c.f. 12:7-8; 13:3-4). Hagar was treated as slave and property to be used and misused by her mistress and master but God treated differently and appeared to Hagar with a promise and assurance. In this part of story, there is a dark side and a bright side. The dark side is Sarah's mistreatment and the bright side is the voice of the Angel of the Lord.[288]

---

[283] Sarah instead of calling Hagar turns to Abraham. It sounds like Sarah is placing the legal custom before Abraham to judge and vindicate her case.

[284] The Hebrew word used here is *'ānâh*. The same word is used in Exodus 1:11-12. It refers for oppression.

[285] The Angel of the Lord gave Hagar two sure words (Hortatory-return and submit and promissory-she would give birth to a son) [See Allen, 56].

[286] God heard the misery of Hagar, the Egyptian similar to the misery of Israel in Egyptian bondage.

[287] Hagar named the place 'Beer Lahai Roi' which means God the one who sees me. God is the one who hears and sees the cry of the needy and oppressed.

[288] Allen P. Ross, "Genesis," 56. For Gordon J. Wenham, 'Hagar comes out best in the end. She becomes Abraham's wife. She receives divine promise. And

In the second part of the story, Abraham arranged a great feast on the day that Isaac was weaned. This act of celebration is not seen in the case of Ishmael. Sarah saw the son of Hagar the Egyptian mocking[289] her son Isaac. Seeing this, Sarah said to Abraham, 'Cast out *this* slave woman with *her son*, for the *son of this slave woman* shall not be heir with *my son Isaac*.' In this statement we could notice the strong word play, a word play of differentiation: 'This slave' and 'her son,' and 'son of this slave woman' and 'my son Isaac.' This differentiation was not seen in the initial stage of plan (Gen. 16: 1-2 'I shall obtain children by her'). Like the first part of the story, Abraham though knew that Ishmael is his son failed to mediate between the two women. Abraham after hearing the word of God decided to send both Hagar and the child with bread and a skin of water. Hagar instead of responding to the decision of betrayal moved out once again to the wilderness (Gen. 21:8-14). God who appeared to Hagar in the wilderness on the way to Shur (Gen. 16:7) appeared to her once again in the wilderness of Beersheba (Gen. 21:17). God again gave her a promise 'I will make him a great nation.' The promise is similar to the promise given to Abraham[290] (Gen 21:18 c.f. Gen. 12:2a). In addition to this great promise, the presence of God with the Lad is mentioned (Gen. 21:20).

In all these events, the role of Hagar was not of center but of margin. In both parts of the story, the angel of the Lord/God appeared to Hagar with words of promise and assurance. It shows clearly that God is not only the 'God of Center' but also 'God of Margins.' He hears the desperate cries of the downtrodden and

---

eventually she bears a son not for Sarah as was planned (Gen.16:2) but as the narrator says three times (Gen.16:15-16) for Abraham.' Refer Gordon J. Wenham, "Genesis 16-50," in *Word Biblical Commentary*, ed. David A. Hubbard and Glenn W. Barker, Vol. 2 (Texas: Word Books, 1994), 4.

[289] We could see a word play over here. The meaning of Isaac is 'laughter' and the word for mocking is *m̊ṣaḥēq* means 'laughter.' Sarah mistreated Hagar in Genesis 16 and in Genesis 21 Ishmael is mistreating Isaac. In both parts of the story Sarah was instrumental in chasing out. In Genesis 16 Hagar was chased out and in chapter 21, Hagar and her son [Allen, 62].

[290] Hagar became a matriarch 'mother of a great nation' as Abraham became a Patriarch 'father of a great nation' (c.f. Gen 12 and 21).

abandoned ones.[291] God hears (Gen. 21:17a), speaks (Gen. 21:17b), acts (Gen. 21:19) and lives (Gen. 21:20) with the downtrodden and marginalized group (c.f. Exod 2:23-25; 3:7-12).

Hannah and Peninnah: Center and Margin

The Book of Samuel must be read against the background of the book of Judges. The book of Judges is considered as a period of anarchy. The people did what was right in their own eyes as there was no king (Judges 21:25). During this period, the narrator is highlighting about a family named Elkanah.[292] He had two wives. Hannah was the first wife and Peninnah the second wife. Peninnah had children and Hannah had no children (I Sam 1:2). The names of the wives draw their role in the family. Hannah means charming and attractive indicates her role as an individual whom Elkannah loved. Peninnah means fertile or prolific indicating her identity as child bearer.[293] Though Hannah was loved by her husband but she was barren. The covenant community though loved by God was in a barren situation. The main characters in this chapter are two women: Hannah and Peninnah.

The question before us is: Who is playing the role of Center and Margin? Hannah or Peninnah.

Hannah: Center or Margin

Hannah was the favorite wife of Elkanah. Though Elkanah comes from the priestly family, he followed the common custom of

---

[291] Jesudason Baskar Jeyaraj, "Genesis,"38.

[292] Elkanah is addressed as an Ephramite. He was a direct descendant of Levi (I Chron 6:33-38) and was therefore qualified to functioned as a priest. He was Levite by lineage but an Ephramite by residence [Eugene H. Merrill, "I Samuel," in *Bible Knowledge Commentary*, ed. John F. Walvoord and Roy B. Zuck (Hyderabad: Authentic Books, 2012), 433].

[293] Bruce C. Birch, "The First and Second Books of Samuel," in *The New Interpreter's Bible*, ed. Leander E. Keck, Vol. 2 (Nashville: Abingdon Press, 1988), 973-974. Also refer Ralph W. Klein, "I Samuel," in *Word Biblical Commentary*, ed. David A. Hubbard and Glen W. Barker, Vol.10 (Texas: Word Books, 1983), 6.

polygamy[294] instead of waiting upon God. He followed the norm of the day: 'In those days every man did that which was right in the sight of his own eyes.' As Sarah urged Abraham to have a son through her maid Hagar, Hannah who was barren may have urged her husband to take another wife.[295] Like Sarah who failed to wait, Hannah too failed to wait. Unlike the Sarah-Hagar episode of free and bond women, here both Hannah and Peninnah are free. Peninnah bore Elkanah several children. Since Hannah was loved by Elkanah, Peninnah grieved Hagar with her tongue.[296] The agony of Hannah became more intense as day progressed. More than barrenness, her rival's jealousy and heartlessness burdened her. Though Hannah is first wife and her husband loved her more than her rival, she unlike Sarah decided to keep her sanctity, controlled her emotion over her sorrow, and poured out her heart before God resulting to joyous and buoyant moment. It finally led to thanksgiving song. The song was so messianic in character that Mary, the mother of Jesus, incorporated it into her own song of triumph which is known as 'Magnificat' (Luke 1:46-55).[297]

Though Hannah is in the center,[298] but she decided to play the role of margin (to be silent). When her rival kept provoking her

---

[294] Polygamy was not forbidden but was bound to lead to domestic discord, especially where one was childless. It is the bitterest fortune possible for an Eastern Woman. Refer Laurence E. Porter, "I and 2 Samuel," in *New International Bible Commentary*, ed. F. F. Bruce, H.L. Ellison and G. C. D. Howley (Grand Rapids, Michigan: Zondervan Publishing House, 1979), 354. Hans Wilhem Hertzberg, *I and II Samuel: A Commentary* (Philadelphia: The Westminster Press, 1964), 23.

[295] Herbert Lockyer, *All the Women of the Bible*, 64-65. In Ancient West Asia, having an heir was very important, for lacking an heir meant the end of one's house. This is seen also in South Asian context (David Toshio Tsumara, *The First Book of Samuel* (Grand Rapids, Michigan: William B. Eerdmans Publishing Company, 2007), 108.

[296] In verse 6, the Hebrew word *gam* is used. The force of *gam* i.e., indeed is to suggest that this is an additional hardship placed on Hannah to provoke her to anger and to irritate her. Refer P. Kyle McCarter Jr. *The Anchor Bible: I Samuel* (New York: Double day, 1980), 52.

[297] Eugene H. Merrill, "I Samuel," 434.

[298] Tsumara quotes C. Meyers saying 'The narrative of Samuels' birth could just as well as be called the Hannah narrative' (David Toshio Tsumara, *The First*

in order to irritate her and to make her cry, Hannah unlike Sarah decided not to retaliate or pressurize Elkanah to chase her out.[299] She decided to cast herself entirely on the mercies of God. Even in the sanctuary of God she opted for a silent prayer (I Sam 1:13). Her silent prayer was so intense that Eli, the high priest noted the movement of her lips and assumed her as a drunken woman. Hannah protested her innocence[300] and declared that she had never taken drink rather pouring out her soul to the Lord.[301] Her dignified approach won the heart of Eli and God. She received the words of assurance by Eli 'Go in Peace, and may the God of Israel grant you what you have asked of Him (I Sam 1:17).'[302] She was no longer sorrow and downcast. God remembered her and granted her wish by giving her a son named Samuel meaning 'asked of the Lord.'[303]

Peninnah: Center or Margin

Peninnah the second wife of Elkanah is described as a rival, a term seldom used in describing family relationships and often translated as 'enemy/adversary' in describing relationships between peoples or nations.[304] Peninnah was jealous because Hannah was loved by Elkanah. She used her fertility to lord it over her rival.[305] Hannah's

---

Book of Samuel, 108).

[299] In the book of Genesis we can see the jealousy which Jacob's bigamy wrought in Rachel's heart (Genesis 30:1).

[300] Silence doesn't mean not to protest. Her protest was in a dignified manner.

[301] Herbert Lockyer, *All the Women of the Bible*, 66-67. The expression 'pouring out my soul' denotes not simply an inward state of one's heart or mind but an involvement of the whole being' (David Toshio Tsumara, *The First Book of Samuel*, 121).

[302] Hannah's approach towards misjudgment of Eli was so modest that Eli believes her without a fraction of doubt resulting not only to offer a word of peace but also consoles and offer a word of promise leading to fulfilment (refer Hans Wilhem Hertzberg, *I and II Samuel: A Commentary*, 25).

[303] Samuel comes from two Hebrew word meaning 'name of God' i.e., he over whom the name of God has been said (see Hans Wilhem Hertzberg, *I and II Samuel: A Commentary*, 25).

[304] Bruce C. Birch, "The First and Second Books of Samuel," 878-879.

[305] Ralph W. Klein, *I Samuel*, 7.

barrenness overrides the power of Elkanah's love.[306] The outcome grieved Hannah with Peninnah's scurrilous tongue. The antagonizing of Peninnah was so intense that none of the Elkanah's assurances had any beneficial effect upon Hannah. Here Peninnah is playing the role of Center by belittling her rival Hannah.

The climax of Hannah-Peninnah episode is different from Sarah-Hagar episode. In the latter case, Sarah playing the role of center succeeded in chasing out Hagar whereas in the former case, Hannah decided to play the role of silence and won the race over Peninnah, the Center. The story ends with a song and a successful judge Samuel (I Sam.3:19-20). In Sarah-Hagar episode, God heard the misery of Hagar and the cry of the lad provided the immediate need with promise of descendants. In Hannah-Peninnah episode, God through Eli assured message of blessings in the form of a successful judge Samuel.

Conclusion

In this chapter, we have seen two episodes, the episode of Sarah-Hagar and the episode of Hannah and Peninnah. In the episode of Sarah-Hagar, Sarah played the role of Center asking her husband Abraham to have a son for her through her maid Hagar. And it is Sarah who compelled Abraham to drive her out from the house. Hagar played the role of margin. As a property and having no rights, she yielded to the demand of her mistress. In the end of the story, God appeared to the margin Hagar and assured protection to her lad and promised to make her seed into a great nation. In the episode of Hannah and Peninnah, both are free women. Their family connections are not stated. Hannah being the first wife is legally in a higher position and Peninnah on a lower position. The fertility aspect made Peninnah to lord over Hannah. Hannah unlike Sarah took an alternative approach. She decided to share her petition before God resulting to a promise of a son. Her approach of not responding or retaliating to her rival and her modest response to the misjudged priest Eli bears the stamp of truth in her. Eli believes her completely by offering

---

306 Walter Brueggemann, *First and Second Samuel* (Louisiville: John Knox Press, 1990), 3.

words of peace, consoles and promises the fulfillment of her request leading to a song of thanksgiving. And her rival Peninnah disappears from the scene. The end of the story is Hannah translated her status from margin (I Samuel 1) to center (I Samuel 2-3).

Chapter 6

Exodus Story: God of the Margins

Re-Reading the Paradigmatic Event from a Margin Perspective

The Exodus event is of paramount importance to the people of ancient Israel as it is a victory story. It is considered as God's greatest act of salvation in the Hebrew Bible.[307] For George Edayadiyil, "Exodus event is the foundational event that shaped the people of Israel in all its history."[308] It is the foundational event that shaped almost all people's movements in theological circles. All these movements are highly indebted to the Exodus event as it recounts the liberation of Israelites under Moses (people of margin) from Pharaoh and his army (people of center). The event is seen as an open contest between Yahweh (Promise of seeds-Genesis chapters

---

[307] Raymond B. Dillard and Tremper Longman III, *An Introduction to the Old Testament* (England: Intervarsity Press, 1995), 65.

[308] George Edayadiyil, *Exodus Event: Its Historical Event* (Bangalore: Asian Trading Corporation, 2007), 1. The exodus event has dual aspects: liberation and formation. It points out the liberation from Egypt and formation of the people through the wilderness and entry into Canaan for a settled life (See Edayadiyil, *Exodus Event: Its Historical Event*, 2.

12, 15, and 17) and Pharaoh (Killer of seeds-Exodus chapter 1 and 2). The victory is often credited to Moses. But, a closer reading of Exodus reveals unsung groups who were instrumental in the liberation act along with Moses. These groups can be categorized as the 'Margins' whose *modus operandi* was 'power-with-others' rather 'power-over-others.'

This chapter is an attempt to bring out the unrecognized and silent figures among the margins who contributed immensely in the liberation of the covenant community.

Background Studies

The story of ancient Israel is connected with a series of connecting links which can be termed as 'covenant.' The word covenant comes from a Hebrew word *Berit*. It is an agreement between two unequal parties, the higher and the lower party. Unlike the covenant treaty of neighboring nations where lower party approaches the higher party to seal an agreement, the Bible reverses the order. The covenant God approaches the lower party 'the covenant people' in spite of their drawbacks. We could locate series of covenants in the Hebrew Bible namely Adamic covenant (Genesis 3), Noahic covenant (Genesis 9), Abrahamic covenant (Genesis 12, 15), Mosaic covenant (Exodus 19), Davidic Covenant (II Samuel 7) and New covenant (Jeremiah 31). The Exodus event took place between the Abrahamic and Mosaic covenant.

The Abrahamic covenant can be best understood against the backdrop of Genesis 3-11 where series of fall can be seen namely Adam and Eve's disobedience to the creator God, Cain killing his own brother, sin of the community during Noah's time and the rebellious act of people by erecting Tower of Babel. Against this backdrop, God called Abraham with a series of promises. The fulfillment of promises will depend on Abraham's obedience towards the call (Genesis 12:1-4). During the course of journey Abraham and Sarah perhaps in their stay in Egypt acquired an Egyptian maid Hagar. Sarah in order to have a child gave Hagar to Abraham. The maid and her child in the course of time were chased out from the home to wilderness. God visited them with promises. After a while, the third generation of Abraham moved to Egypt for survival ending up in slavery. Their life situation became like the situation of Hagar who was acquired from Egypt. During the time of slavery, the people of Israel cried unto the Lord. God, who heard the cry of Hagar and her child, heard the cry of the Israelites. He came down and rescued His people through a group of His chosen ones which includes Moses. Just like Andrew who was instrumental in leading his brother Peter to Jesus, many women were instrumental in saving Moses who in turn with the help of his people and with the divine intervention of God saved the covenant community from Pharaoh and his army. The saving act of God lead to a covenant known as Mosaic covenant (Exodus 19).

Exodus Story: Battle between Yahweh/Margins and Pharaoh/Center

God in His divine plan called Abraham from the land of Ur to the land of Canaan with promises. The promises of God to Abraham were mainly two-fold: Progeny and Land. It started in a low phase with series of challenges and oppositions. In due course, the promise of progeny was fulfilled (Exod. 1:7). In a period of time there arose a new king over Egypt who did not know Joseph. Seeing the growth of Israel and being afraid and suspicious of them, the king passed an order to deal shrewdly with them. But the more they were oppressed, the more they multiplied and the more they multiplied they spread. The king at last decided to kill the male child (Exodus 1:15-16, 22). A careful reading reveals as a contest between Yahweh, the proclaimer of promises and Pharaoh, the destroyer of promise. The proclaimer in order to execute appointed Moses as the leader. Though it is acknowledged by many that Moses was leader par excellence but there were a few who too played active role in the life and mission of Moses.

Heroic Acts of Women: Outside-Inside Partnering

Throughout the Bible, we could see the heroic act of women namely Rahab, Hannah, Deborah, Ruth, Esther etc. In the Exodus event too, there are number of women namely the midwives, Jochebed,

Miriam and Pharaoh's daughter.[309] We often give credit to Moses and Joshua, but a closer reading reveals the crucial role of women in preparing the way of deliverance and blessings. These five women are 'Women of Margins.' They are 'Outside-Inside' women facing the order of Pharaoh whose word is considered as a law. Disobeying the law of Pharaoh will attract capital punishment. The battle was not a battle between God and Pharaoh; it also became a battle between the center and the margins.

Role of Margins: Adopting Different Paths

All these five women took different paths to foil the dictating order of the mighty Pharaoh.

Midwives: The Middle Path

There are differences of opinion regarding Hebrew midwives, whether the midwives are Hebrew midwives or midwives of the Hebrew women. If Hebrew midwives, how Pharaoh can expect them to carry out the genocide of their own people? If it is midwives of the Hebrew women, it opens up the possibility that they were Egyptians and are expected to comply with the king's diabolic demands.[310] In my understanding, the midwives were Hebrew or Egyptian who embraced Hebrew faith as the text clearly says that they feared God.

---

[309] It is quite interesting to note that in the first two chapters of Exodus other than the midwives (named as Shiprah and Puah), no one else is mentioned by name. They are addressed with their male counterpart (wife a daughter of Levi, his sister, daughter of Pharaoh).

[310] Robert P. Gordon, "Exodus," in *New International Bible Commentary*, ed. F. F. Bruce (Grand Rapids, Michigan: Zondervan Publishing House, 1979), 155-156. According to Herbert Lockyer, Puah and Shiprah are Egyptian names. She quoting Aben Ezra, the ancient Jewish historian, says that these two women were chiefs over all the midwives who were more than 500. Although Egyptian by birth, it would seem as if they had embraced the Hebrew faith (Exod. 1:21) [see Herbert Lockyer, *All the Women of the Bible* (Secunderabad: OM Books, 1967), 126].

Reading the text makes clear that the Hebrew midwives Shiprah[311] and Puah[312] are not defying the order of Pharaoh[313] openly and not even taking the stand by saying that they will protect the Hebrew infants. They decided to take a middle path. When Pharaoh summoned them for their misconduct, the midwives answered tactfully. Thinking fast they said that we couldn't help it, because unlike Egyptian women,[314] the Hebrew women delivered so quickly[315] that before they arrive, the babies were already delivered. Their story looks convincing as the Israelite women were in harsh conditions leading to quick delivery.[316] Perhaps the king was induced with their response and did not punish them for their inability to execute the policy. God honored for their courage of faith by building them houses/families. Their names became part of salvation history.[317]

Jochebed: The Silent Judicious Path

Jochebed approach was silent but a judicious approach to preserve the life of her baby boy. She decided to make a papyrus basket coated with tar and pitch and placed the basket in the marsh. It is quite ironic to note the fact that she obeyed the edict of Pharaoh by putting the basket in the Nile River.[318] However, she did differently. Instead of

---

311 Fair one.

312 Fragrant one.

313 For John Durham, Pharaoh applied three plans to control the strength and growth of the children of Israel. Plan A was to increase workload; plan B was murderous plan; and plan C was more drastic and violent one (John I Durham, "Exodus," in *Word Biblical Commentary*, ed. Bruce M. Metzger, David A. Hubbard and Glenn W. Barker, Vol. 3 (Columbia: Nelson Reference, 1987), 11.

314 For Durham, 'the quick reply of the midwives to Pharaoh's question is tinged with wit. Not only the Hebrew women robust delivering and caring for their babies themselves with a minimum of bother and self-indulgence-the Egyptian women are just the opposite (See John I Durham, "Exodus," 12).'

315 Robust.

316 Robert P. Gordon, "Exodus,"156.

317 P. G. George and Paul Swarup, "Exodus," in *South Asia Bible Commentary*, ed. Brian Wintle (Udaipur: Open Door Publications Ltd., 2015), 80.

318 John D. Hannah, "Exodus," in *The Bible Knowledge Commentary*, ed. John F. Walvoord and Roy B. Zuck (Hyderabad: Authentic, 2010), 109.

throwing the baby in the Nile River, she placed in a basket and that too in the exact location where Pharaoh's daughter will come for a bath.[319] In order to execute the plan, she perhaps asked her daughter to watch the movement. Miriam's question to Pharaoh's daughter clearly indicates the clever stratagem of Jochebed.[320] Throughout the event Jochebed is not uttering rather acting wisely to make sure the things fall in its place.

Jochebed as carries the name 'Glory of Yahweh/Yahweh is her Glory,' was instrumental in upbringing all her three children in the liberation of the people of Israel from the bondage of Egypt. Moses played the role of liberator and law giver. Aaron became Israel's first high priest and the founder of the Aaronic priesthood. Miriam, the talented poetess and musician was intimately connected with her two brothers in the process of liberation and national identity. Her contribution in the liberation process resulted in rich dividend as her name is placed among the heroines of faith in Hebrews (Hebrews 11:23).[321] In all these events, the text is not mentioning the words of Jochebed but acts of Jochebed, i.e., silent but clever act.

Miriam: The Clever Path

Miriam perhaps taking the advice of her mother watched from a distance. She closely observed Pharaoh's daughter. Reading and realizing the compassionate attitude of Pharaoh's daughter, without wasting the time quickly responded for an offer to have a nurse among the Hebrew women. Lockyer beautifully states, 'Out of the shadows she stepped forth so innocently, and appearing to be curious

---

[319] For Durham, the placing of basket in the river was not a deliberate one as it will harm the baby. It was unintended and dangerous. The delight of the discovery is the totally unexpected way it turned out. The climax of the discovery is the quick and bold action of the little boy's sister (See John I Durham, "Exodus," 16).

[320] Herbert Lockyer, *All the Women of the Bible*, 80. According to Lockyer, God through the intensity of her faith caused her to inherit a vision of what he had appointed for Moses. She made a little cradle to protect against crocodiles and then placed the cradle with its treasure secretly among the rushes at the river's bank and told her daughter to watch over it.

[321] Herbert Lockyer, *All the Women of the Bible*, 79- 80. Jochebed is the first person in the Bible to have a name compounded with *Jah* (Yahweh).

at the screaming baby and puzzled princess, ask if she would like her to find a Hebrew nurse. Miriam kept her silence and did not reveal her relation to the baby and the nurse she secured.'[322] Her timely words and the wise step show the intelligence of a small girl Miriam aged 10-12 years. She was instrumental in reuniting the child with his mother. The mother was remunerated for her service.

In the later chapter, we could see the song of Miriam (Exod. 15:20-21) along with the praise of Moses. She became the first woman in the Bible to be called as a prophetess. Prophet Micah of eighth century B.C.E marked her contribution along with Moses and Aaron as leaders in the life journey of Israel (Micah 6:4- 'I brought you up out of Egypt and redeemed you from the land of slavery. I sent Moses to lead you also Aaron and Moses).

Lockyer in her work quoting Josephus (*Antiquities*) states that Miriam became the wife of another well-known leader in Israel namely Hur, one of the judges of the people when Moses was on Mount Sinai (Exod. 24:14). This would make Miriam to be the grandmother of Bezalel, the famous artist in the construction of the Tabernacle (Exod. 31:2).[323]

Pharaoh's Daughter: The Bold Path

Pharaoh's daughter knowing the fact that her father has passed the edict to throw every Hebrew boy into the river Nile risked her own life. She decided to save the child from the river, named the child, adopted the child when the child grew older (1:22, 2:5-10) and raised the child as her own son in the palace for 40 long years. The child in turn became the liberator of Israel.

It is reasonable to agree with the fact that both Jochebed and Miriam through their sheer intelligence were able to save their own blood Moses. But it often puzzles, what made Pharaoh's daughter to go differently from her father? Though she was an Egyptian but carried the heart of a mother. By doing so she superseded both her

---

[322] Herbert Lockyer, *All the Women of the Bible*, 112.

[323] Herbert Lockyer, *All the Women of the Bible*, 111. The Scripture however indicates that Miriam remained in single blessedness all her days.

father and the negative character in Genesis (Potiphar's wife). She felt it is too cruel to murder the little baby. She had a spirit of humanity.[324]

God and the People of Margins

It is quite interesting to note that all women mentioned in chapter two are anonymous. Their name is attached to the male counterparts.[325] Though their name is anonymous but their initiative and action was closely connected. Jochebed was guided by God to make a small cradle to place her son and to place it among the reeds. Miriam was there to make sure her brother is in safe hand. Pharaoh's daughter was also ordered by the same God to raise the child to be acquainted with the Egyptian system to deliver the people of Israel from the imperial power of Egypt. Jochebed *out of the reeds* grown along the banks of the river fashioned a small boat to keep baby Moses. Miriam *out of the shadows* stepped forth to reunite her brother with her mother. Pharaoh's daughter *out of the water* drew the baby and called him Moses.[326] Moses in turn took the people of Israel *out of the land* of Egypt. Behind all these stages of event, though there is no reference to God, but His sovereign plan is unraveled as He prepared the people of margins to defy the plan and strategy of the center.

Conclusion

The paths of margins are a progressive path building upon each other. When Pharaoh, the Center ordered a decree to kill Hebrew male child, the women folk, people of margins decided to take different paths to prepare the liberator Moses. The midwives took a middle path, Jochebed took a silent but judicious path, Miriam took a clever path and Pharaoh's daughter took a bold path. All these paths in turn helped Moses to lead the people from the land of bondage/slavery to the land of milk and honey.

---

[324] Herbert Lockyer, *All the Women of the Bible*, 178-179.

[325] Jochebed is mentioned as 'daughter of Levi,' Miriam is mentioned as 'his sister,' and daughter of Pharaoh (Exodus 2:1, 4, 5).

[326] For Durham, 'The medium of death becomes for Moses the medium of life. His life is moved from danger to privilege. Moses enjoys the best of both worlds possible to him (See John I Durham, "Exodus," 16).'

Bibliography

Anderson, Cherly B. *Ancient Laws and Contemporary Controversies.* Oxford: Oxford University Press, 2009.

Anderson, Cheryl B. *Women, Ideology and Violence: Critical Theory and the Construction of the Gender in the Book of the Covenant and the Deuteronomic Law*. London: T& T Clark, 2004.

Balentine, Samuel E."Leviticus," in *Interpretation*, ed. Patrick D. Miller. Louisville: John Knox Press, 2002.

Bendor-Samuel, John "Esther," in *New International Bible Commentary,* ed. F. F. Bruce. Grand Rapids, Michigan: Zondervan, 1979.

Bernstein, Moshe J, "Two Multivalent readings in the Ruth narrative," *JSOT* 50 (1991): 15-26.

Berquist, J. L., "Role differentiation in the Book of Ruth," *JSOT* 57 (1993): 23-37.

Berquist, Jon L *Judaism in Persian's Shadow: A Social and Historical Approach*. Eugene, Origen: Wipf and Stock Publishers, 1995.

Bickerman, Elias *Four Strange Books of the Bible.* New York: Schocken Books, 1967.

Birch, Bruce C. "The First and Second Books of Samuel," in *The New Interpreter's Bible,* ed. Leander E. Keck, Vol.2. Nashville: Abingdon Press, 1988.

Bird, Phyllis "The Place of Women in the Israelite Cultus," in *Ancient Israelite Religion*, Miller Patrick (ed.), Philadelphia: Fortress Press, 1987.

Boss, Johanna W. H., "Out of the shadows: Genesis 38; Judges 4:17-22; Ruth 3," *Semeia*, 42 (1988):37-67.

Breneman, Mervin "Esther," in *An Exegetical and theoretical exposition of the Holy Scripture: Ezra, Nehemiah and Esther*, ed. L. Ray Clandenen, Vol.10. USA: Broadman Holman Publishers, 1993.

Bush, Frederic, "Ruth," *WBC*, Vol.9. Dallas: Word Books Publishers, 1996.

Bush, Fredrich "Esther," in *Word Biblical Commentary: Ruth and Esther*, ed. David A. Hubbard and Glen W. Barker, Vol.9. Dallas: Word Books, 1996.

Campbell Jr., Edward F. , Ruth, *ABC*, Vol.7. New York: Doubleday, 1975.

Cassuto, U. *A Commentary on the Book of Exodus*. Jerusalem: The Magness Press, 1967.

Chakravorty Spivak, Gayatri, "Subaltern Studies: Deconstructing Historiography," in *The Spivak Reader*, ed. Donna Landry and Gerald MacLean. New York: Routledge, 1996.

Childs, Brevard S. *The Book of Exodus*. London: SCM Press, 1974.

Chirichigno, Gregory C.. *Debt-Slavery in Israel and the Ancient Near East*, Journal for the Study of the Old Testament Supplement Series 141. Sheffield: Sheffield Academic Press, 1993.

Christensen, Duane L. "Deuteronomy 1:1-21:9," in *Word Biblical Commentary*, ed. John D. W. Watts. Nashville: Thomas Nelson Publishers, 2001.

Chu, Julie L. C, "Returning Home: The inspiration of the role differentiation in the Book of Ruth for Taiwanese Women," *Semeia*, 78 (1997): 47-54.

Clarence, David "Exodus," in *South Asia Bible Commentary*, ed. Brian Wintle. Udaipur: Open Door Publication, 2015.

Clements, R. E. "Deuteronomy," in *Old Testament Guides*, ed. R. N. Whybray. Sheffield: JSOT Press, 1989.

Clements, Ronald E. *Exodus*. Cambridge: Cambridge University Press, 1972.

Clines, David J. A. *The Esther Scroll*. Sheffield: JSOT Press, 1984.

Coxon, Peter W, "Was Naomi a Scold?: A Response to Fewell and Gunn," *JSOT* 45 (1989): 25-37.

Craige, Peter C. *The Book of Deuteronomy*. Grand Rapids, Michigan: William B. Eerdmans Publishing Company, 1976.

Crawford, Sidnie White "The Book of Esther," in *The New Interpreter's Bible,* ed. Leander E. Keck, Vol.3. Nashville: Abingdon Press, 1990.

Cunliffe-Jones, H. "Deuteronomy," in *Torch Bible Commentaries,* ed. Alan Richardson John Marsh, R. Gregor Smith. London: SCM Press Ltd, 1951.

Daube, D. *Studies in Biblical Law*. Cambridge: Cambridge University Press, 1947.

Davies, G. Henton *Exodus*. London: SCM Press, 1967.

Dillard, Raymond B and Tremper Longman III, *An Introduction to the Old Testament*. England: Intervarsity Press, 1995.

Donaldson, Laura E, "The sign of Orpah: Reading through native eyes," *Vernacular Hermeneutics,* ed. R. S. Sugirtharajah. Sheffield: Sheffield Academic Press, 1999.

Douglas, Mary *Purity and Danger*. London: Routledge, 1966.

Driver, S. R. "Deuteronomy: A Critical and Exegetical Commentary," in *The International Critical Commentary*, ed. A. Plummer and C. A. Briggs S. R. Driver. Edinburgh: T&T Clark, 1996.

Driver, S. R. *A Critical and Exegetical Commentary on Deuteronomy*. Edinburgh: T&T Clark, 1902.

Durham, John I. "Exodus," in *Word Biblical* Commentary, ed. John D. W. Watts and James W. Watts, 3. USA: Nelson Reference and Electronic, 1987.

Dutcher-Walls, Patrica, "The Social Location of the Deuteronomist: A Sociological study of factional politics in late pre-exilic Judah," *JSOT* 52 (1991): 77-94.

Edayadiyil, George *Exodus Event: Its Historical Event*. Bangalore: Asian Trading Corporation, 2007.

Emmerson, G. I. "Women in Ancient Israel," in *The World of Ancient Israel: Sociological, Anthropological and Political Perspectives,* ed. R. E. Clement. Cambridge: Cambridge University Press, 1989.

Evans, Mary J., *Woman in the Bible*. Devon: The Patemoster Press, 1983.

Fewell, Danna Nolan, "Feminist reading of the Hebrew Bible: Affirmation, Resistance and Transformation," *JSOT* 39 (1987): 77-87.

Fox, Michael V. *Character and Ideology in the Book of Esther*. Grand Rapids, Michigan: William B. Eerdmans Publishing Company, 1991.

Frankfort, Henri *Kingship and the Gods: A Study of Ancient Near Eastern Religion as the integration of society and nature*. Chicago: The University of Chicago press, 1965.

George, Alexi E. "Leviticus," in *South Asia Bible Commentary*. ed. Brian Wintle. Udaipur: Open Door Publications, 2015.

George, P. G. and Paul Swarup, "Exodus," in *South Asia Bible Commentary*, ed. Brian Wintle. Udaipur: Open Door Publications Ltd., 2015.

Gingrich, F. Wilbur and William F. Arndy *A Greek-English Lexicon of the New Testament and Other Early Christian Literature*. Chicago: The University of Chicago Press, 1957.

Gordon, Robert P. "Exodus," in *New International Bible Commentary*, ed. F. F. Bruce. Grand Rapids, Michigan: Zondervan Publishing House, 1979.

Gorman, Frank H. "Divine Presence and Community: A Commentary on the Book of Leviticus," in *International Theological* Commentary, ed. Fredrick Carlson Holmgren and George A. F. Knight. Edinburgh: The Handsel Press, 1997.

Gow, Murray D, *The Book of Ruth: Its Structure, Theme and Purpose.* Leicester: Intervarsity Press, 1992.

Gramsci, Antonio *Selection from Prison Notebooks,* trans. Quintin Hoare and Geoffrey Nowell Smith. London: Lawrence and Wishart, 1978.

Grossman, Jonathan, "Gleaning among the Ears"- "Gathering among the Sheaves": Characterizing the Image of the Supervising Boy (Ruth 2), *JBL,* 126, no.4 (2007): 703-716.

Guha, Ranajit "Preface," in *Subaltern Studies I: Writings on South Asian History and Society,* ed. Ranajit Guha. New Delhi, 1982.

Habel, N. C. "The Future of Social Justice Researching the Hebrew Scriptures: Questions of Authority and Relevance," in *Old Testament Interpretation: Past, Present and Future.* London: T & T Clark, 1995.

Hals Ronald M, *The Theology of the Book of Ruth.* Philadelphia: Fortress Press, 1969.

Hannah, John D. "Exodus," in *The Bible Knowledge Commentary,* ed. John F. Walvoord and Roy B. Zuck Hyderabad: Authentic, 2010.

Hartley, John E. "Leviticus," in *Word Biblical Commentary,* ed. John D. W. Watts, 4. Texas: Word Books, 1992.

Hertzberg, Hans Wilhem *I and II Samuel: A Commentary.* Philadelphia: The Westminster Press, 1964.

Houtman, Cornelis "Exodus," in *Historical Commentary on the Old Testament,* ed. Gert T. M. Prinsloo Cornelis Houtman, Wilfred G. E. Watson and Al Wolters. Leuven: Peeters, 2000.

Huey, F. B., "Ruth," *The Expositor's Bible Commentary,* ed. Frank E. Gaebelein, Vol.3. Michigan: Zondervan Publishing House, 1992.

Humphreys, W. Lee "The Rise and Fall of King Saul: A Study of Ancient Narrative Stratum in I Samuel," *JSOT* 18 (1980): 74-90.

Hyatt, J. P. *Exodus.* London: Oliphants, 1971.

Isser, Stanley "Two Traditions: The Law of Exodus 21:22-23 Revisited," *The Catholic Biblical Quarterly* 52 (1990):30-45.

Jesurathnam, K. "Dalit and Subaltern Hermeneutics in Conversation with Reader Response Method: I Kings 22, A Case in Point," *Bangalore Theological Forum* 1 (2016): 46-60.

Jeyaraj, Jesudason Baskar "Genesis," in *South Asia Bible Commentary*, ed. Brian Wintle. Udaipur: Open Door Publications, 2015.

Joy, C. I. David "The Social and Religious Origins of the Gospel of Mark and Its Hermeneutical Implications: A Post-Colonial Critique," *Bangalore Theological Forum* 33, no. 1 (2001): 1-24.

Kaiser, Walter C "The Book of Leviticus," in *The New Interpreter's Bible*, ed. Leander E. Keck. Nashville: Abingdon Press, 1994.

Kaufmann, Yehezkel *The Religion of Israel: From its Beginnings to the Babylonian Exile*. London: George Allen & Unwin Ltd., 1960.

Keck, Leander E. (ed.),"The Book of Ruth," *TNIB*, Vol.2. Nashville: Abingdon Press, 1988.

Keil, C. F. "The Pentateuch," in *Commentary on the Old Testament*, ed. C. F. Keil and F. Delitzsch. Massachusetts: Hendrickson Publishers, 2001.

Klein, Ralph W. "I Samuel," in *Word Biblical Commentary*, ed. David A. Hubbard and Glen W. Barker, Vol.10. Texas: Word Books, 1983.

Kline, Meredith G. *Treaty of the Great King*. Grand Rapids, Michigan: William B. Eerdmans Publishing Company, 1963.

Lemche, N. P. "The Hebrew Slave: Comments on the Slave Law Exodus 21:2-11," *Vetus Testamentum* 25 (1975): 124-144.

Lemche, N. P. "Manumission of Slaves-the Fallow Year-the Sabbatical Year-the Jubilee Year," *Vetus Testamentum* 26, no. 1 (1976): 38-59.

Levine, Baruch A. "Leviticus," in *The Jewish Publication Society Torah Commentary*, ed. Nahum M. Sarna. Jerusalem: The Jewish Publication Society, 1989.

Lindenberger, James M. "How Much for a Hebrew Slave? The Meaning of Misneh in Deut 15:18- Critical Notes," *JBL* 110, no. 3 (1991): 479-498.

Lockyer, Herbert *All the Women of the Bible*. Secunderabad: OM Books, 1967.

Ludden, David "Introduction: A Brief History of Subaltenity," in *Reading Subaltern Studies: Critical History, Contested Meaning, and the Globalization of South Asia*, ed. David Ludded. Delhi: Permanent Black, 2003.

Maldonado, Robert D, "Reading Malinche Reading Ruth: Towards a hermeneutics of Betrayal," *Semeia* 72 (1995): 91-110.

Masenya, Madipoane J ,"NGWESTI (Bride) The Naomi- Ruth story from an African-South African Woman's perspective," *Journal of Feminist Studies in Religion* 14, No.2 (1998):78-94.

Mathew, Shiju, "Ruth, a Moabite Gentile Woman blessing the Nation Israel: A Subaltern Reading," *New Life Theological Journal* 3 (2013): 69-77.

Mathew, Shiju "Ruth: The Immigrant, a Journey from Moab to Bethlehem," in *Re-imagining Reformation: Essays in Honor of P. G. George*, ed. Y.T.Vinayaraj, Dexter Maben, Woba James. Delhi: ISPCK, 2017.

Matthews, Victor H *Manners and Customs in the Bible*. Massachusetts: Hendrickson Publishers, 1991.

Matthews, Victor H, Bernard M. Levinson, and Tikva Frymer-Kensky. *Gender and Law in the Hebrew Bible and the Ancient Near East*. Sheffield: Sheffield Academic Press, 1998.

Mayes, A. D. H. "Deuteronomy," in *New Century Bible Commentary*, ed. Ronald E. Clements. Grand Rapids, Michigan: Wm. B. Eerdmans Publishing Company, 1979.

McCarter Jr., P. Kyle *The Anchor Bible: I Samuel*. New York: Double day, 1980.

McGee, J. Vemon, *Ruth: The Romance of Redemption*. Illinois: Van KampenPress, 1954.

Merrill, Eugene H. "Deuteronomy," in *The New American Commentary*, ed. E. Ray Clendenen. USA: Broadman & Holman Publishers, 1994.

Merrill, Eugene H. "I Samuel," in *Bible Knowledge Commentary*, ed. John F. Walvoord and Roy B. Zuck. Hyderabad: Authentic Books, 2012.

Meyers, Eric M. and John Rogerson, "Law in ANE and Israel," *The Cambridge Companion to the Bible*, ed. Bruce Chilton. The Cambridge University Press, 1997.

Milgrom, Jacob "Leviticus 1-16," in *The Anchor Bible*, ed. William Foxwell Albright and David Noel Freedman. New York: Doubleday, 1991.

Mondithoka, Santha Kumari "Ruth," in *South Asia Bible Commentary*, ed. Brian Wintle. Udaipur: Open Door Publications, 2015.

Moore, Carey A. *The Anchor Bible: Esther*. New York: Double day & Company, 1971.

Morenz, Siegfried *Egyptian Religion,* translated by Ann E. Keep. London: Methuen & Co. Ltd., 1973.

Morton, Stephen *Gayatri Chakravorty Spivak*. London: Routledge, 2003.

Muthunayagam, Daniel Jones "Cultural Shifts from the Period of Tribal Confederation to Monarchy," *BTF* 32 (2000): 1-14.

Myers, Joseph, *The Linguistic and Literary of the book of Ruth*. Leiden: E. J. Brill, 1995.

Nadar, Sarojini," Subverting Gender and Ethnic assumptions in Biblical narrative voice of Ruth," *Semeia* 74 (1995): 67-74.

Nadar, Sarojni, "A South African Indian Womanist Reading of the character of Ruth," Musa W. Dube (ed.) *Other ways of Reading African Women and the Bible*. Geneva: WCC Publication, 2001.

Neilson, Kirste , *Ruth: A Commentary*. Louisville: John Knox Press, 1997.

Noth, Martin *The History of Israel*. London: Adam and Charles Black, 1960.

Noth, Martin *Exodus*. London: SCM Press, 1962.

Noth, Martin *Leviticus*. Philadelphia: Westminstress Press, 1965.

Philips, Anthony "The Laws of Slavery: Exodus 21:2-11," *JSOT* 30 (1984): 51-66.

Porter, J. R. "Leviticus," in *The Cambridge Bible Commentary*, ed. A. R. C. Leaney P. R. Ackroyd, J. W. Packer. London: Cambridge University Press, 1976.

Porter, Laurence E. "I and 2 Samuel," in *New International Bible Commentary*, ed. F. F. Bruce, H.L. Ellison and G. C. D. Howley. Grand Rapids, Michigan: Zondervan Publishing House, 1979.

Prinsloo, W. S, "The theology of the book of Ruth," *Vetus Testamentum* 30 (1980): 330-341.

Propp, William H. C. "*Exodus 19-40*," in *The Anchor Bible,* ed. William Foxwell Albright and David Noel Freedman. New York: Doubleday, 2006.

Pui-lan, Kwok*, Introducing Asian Feminist Theology*. Sheffield: Sheffield Academic Press, 2000.

Rad, Gerhard von *Genesis: A Commentary*. Philadelphia: The Westminster Press, 1972.

Rad, Gerhard von *Deuteronomy*. London: SCM Press, 1966.

Rao, Chilkuri Vasantha *Ecological and Theological Aspects of Some Animal Laws in the Pentateuch*. Delhi: ISPCK, 2005.

Rashkow, Ilona, "Ruth: The discourse of power and the power of discourse," in *A Feminist Companion to Ruth*, ed. Athalya Brenner. Sheffield: Sheffield Academic press, 1993.

Ringgren, Helmer "Understanding of Kingship in the Ancient West Asia," *TDOT*, Vol.8, ed. G.Johannes Butter Weck. UK: William B. Eerdmans Publishing Company, 1997.

Robert L. Hubbard, "The Book of Ruth," *The New International commentary of the Old Testament*. Michigan: Grand Rapids, 1988.

Rofe, Alexander "Deuteronomy: Issues and Interpretations," in *Old Testament Studies*, ed. David J. Reimer. London: T&T Clark, 2002.

Rooker, Mark F. "Leviticus," in *The New American Commentary*, ed. E. Ray Clendenen. Nashville: Broadman& Holman Publishers, 2000.

Ross, Allen P. *Holiness to the* Lord. Grand Rapids, Michigan: Baker Academic Press, 2002.

Ross, Allen P. "Genesis," in Bible Knowledge Commentary, ed. John F. Walvoord and Roy B. Zuck. Hyderabad: Authentic Books, 2012.

Sarna, Nahum M "Exodus," in *The Jerusalem Publication Society Torah* Commentary, ed. Nahum M. Sarna. Jerusalem: The Jewish Publication Society, 1991.

Scholz, Susanne "The Complexities of 'His' Liberation Talk: A Literary Feminist Reading of the Book of Exodus," in *Exodus to Deuteronomy*, ed. Athalya Brenner. Sheffield: Sheffield Academic Press, 2000.

Setel, Drorah O' Donnel "Exodus," in *Women's Bible Commentary*, ed. Carol A. Newsom and Sharon H. Ringe. Kentucky: John Knox Press, 1998.

Snaith, N. H."Leviticus and Numbers," in *The Century Bible*, ed. H. H. Rowley. London: Thomas Nelson and Sons Ltd, 1967.

Spivak, Gayatri Chakravorty "Postcolonial Theory and Literature," in *New Dictionary of the History of Ideas*, ed. Maryanne Cline Horowitz. London: Gale Cengage Learning, 2005.

Streane, A. W and A. T. Chapman, *The Book of Leviticus*. Cambridge: University Press, 1914.

Thompson, J. A. *Deuteronomy: An Introduction and Commentary*, ed. D. J. Wiseman. England: Inter-Varsity Press, 1974.

Tigay, Jeffrey H. "Deuteronomy," in *The Jewish Publication Society Torah Commentary*, ed. Nahum M. Sarna. Jerusalem: The Jewish Publication Society, 1996.

Trible, Phyllis,"Two women in a Man' world: A reading of the Book of Ruth," *Soundings*, 59 (1976): 252-279.

Tsumara, David Toshio *The First Book of Samuel.* Grand Rapids, Michigan: William B. Eerdmans Publishing Company, 2007.

Vance, Donald R, *A Hebrew Reader for Ruth.* Peabody: Hendrickson Publishers, 2003.

Wallis, Hale G. "Chāmadh," in *Theological Dictionary of the Old Testament,* ed. G. Johannes Botterweck and Helmer Ringgren .Grand Rapids, Michigan: William B. Eerdmans Publishing Company, 1980.

Wansbrough, Henry *Genesis: Doubleday Bible Commentary.* New York: Doubleday, 1998.

Weinfeld, Moshe *Deuteronomy and the Deuteronomic School.* Oxford: Clarendon Press, 1972.

Wells, Bruce "What Is Biblical Law? A Look at Pentateuchal Rules and near Eastern Practice," *The Catholic Biblical* Quarterly 70 (2008): 223-243.

Wenham, Gordon J. "Genesis 16-50," in *Word Biblical Commentary,* ed. David A. Hubbard and Glenn W. Barker, Vol.2.Texas: Word Books, 1994.

Wenham, Gordon J. "The Book of Leviticus," in *The New International Commentary on the Old Testament,* ed. R. K. Harrison. Grand Rapids, Michigan: William B. Eerdmans Publishing Company, 1979.

Wilfred, Felix "Towards a Subaltern Hermeneutics: Beyond the Contemporary Polarities in the Interpretation of Religious Tradition," *Jeeva Dhara* 26, no. 151 (1996): 45-62.

Index of Subjects

N

P

R

S

T

V

Index of Authors